Law School Exams

Law School Exams

A Guide to Better Grades

Alex Schimel

CAROLINA ACADEMIC PRESS
Durham, North Carolina

Library of Congress Cataloging-in-Publication Data

Schimel, Alex
Law school exams : a guide to better grades / Alex Schimel.
    p. cm.
ISBN 978-1-61163-059-6 (alk. paper)
1. Law examinations--United States. 2. Law students--United
States--Handbooks, manuals, etc. I. Title.

KF283.S335 2012
340.076--dc23

                    2011053323

Figures and illustrations courtesy of Spencer Schimel.

CAROLINA ACADEMIC PRESS
700 Kent Street
Durham, North Carolina 27701
Telephone (919) 489-7486
Fax (919) 493-5668
www.cap-press.com

Printed in the United States of America

Contents

Foreword

Joanne Harvest Koren

When I started the Academic Achievement Program (AAP) at the University of Miami School of Law in 1994, I knew I wanted to design the Law School's "pilot" academic support program as one that uses upper level law students as Dean's Fellows (or "teaching assistants"). I thought that if I could find 12 upper level students who were willing to do just as I thought and said, we could design and implement a successful academic support program to serve the needs of our 1L students.

I soon learned how naïve I was in my thinking. After hiring 12 intelligent, dynamic, clever and creative students as Dean's Fellows, I quickly realized they often had different ideas about how things should be taught, planned and done. Happily, I also quickly discovered that this was a very good thing, and I was willing and enthusiastic about incorporating those students' ideas into my own plans. As the program has grown and developed I have depended on the student Dean's Fellows to help me create and shape that initial vision into the successful program it is today.

In the more than sixteen years since I created the program, I have been extremely fortunate to have had the opportunity to hire, train, supervise, work with and get to know hundreds of successful law students who choose to spend a great deal of their 2L and 3L years working with me in the Academic Achievement Program. Among those hundreds of outstanding students, Alex Schimel stands out. He is a remarkably intelligent and creative young man who has innovative ideas and a talent for teaching. In addition, he has the unique ability to make his clever ideas and methods of teaching and learning seem quite straightforward and sensible.

I first met Alex when he was a 1L student. He sent me an email thanking me for presenting a "1L Boot Camp" program at the beginning of the year, which he found very helpful. I invited Alex to come to my office so we could discuss the program. Even as a 1L student, in the second week of class, Alex was insightful, thoughtful and analytical and saw things with a clear and discerning eye. It did not surprise me to learn Alex finished his first year of law school at the top of his class.

In the fall of his second year of law school, Alex began working with me as a Writing Dean's Fellow in the Academic Achievement Program Writing Center. We spent many visits talking about student learning, teaching, exam writing and law school in general. He had observed and participated in the process of "law school learning" and had well-developed and interesting ideas. Although (and perhaps because) Alex's ideas sometimes differed from mine, I thoroughly appreciated his insight and vantage point. I was delighted when Alex offered to assume the role of Dean's Fellow for the Academic Achievement Program's Spring Exam Workshop series. In that role he would have the opportunity to work with fellow students who were trying to find ways to improve their academic experience and acclimate to law study. The weekly AAP Exam Workshop sessions are voluntary, but students are asked to commit to the eight weekly sessions.

In discussing the planning of those sessions with Alex, it became quite evident that he had a theory and program model for exam-taking success. Hundreds of students flocked to the voluntary weekly Exam Workshop sessions Alex taught. Sometimes there was "standing room only" in the classroom. Word got out around the law school and in the two years Alex taught the Exam Workshop, several hundred students benefited from insight into Alex's law school and exam-taking advice. Alex's advice has become somewhat institutionalized here. In fact, around the University of Miami School of Law, current Dean's Fellows and students call Alex's "IRAHNC" method of exam writing the "Schimel Method."

Alex is an excellent and effective teacher. He presents useful and valuable lessons in an entertaining and matter-of fact way. In writing this book, Alex shares his insight and his methods with readers, who will, no doubt, enjoy an experience a similar to that of the students who had the benefit of Alex as a classroom teacher.

Readers of this book are in for a treat. The book offers sensible, practical and comprehensive advice and strategies for students new to law school study and exam taking—and also to students who may have already completed the first or second year of law school and are seeking alternative strategies for greater competency and academic achievement.

There are many books available that offer new law students advice and strategies for success in law school. What makes this book so unique is the vantage point of its author: An intelligent, successful (recently graduated) law student writing a book for fellow law students, offering realistic insight, sound advice and tried and true strategies. The book is sensible, practical, comprehensive and ... funny! In reading the book, the reader hears Alex's voice. It sounds just like Alex does when he speaks. Any law student would be wise to listen.

Joanne Harvest Koren
Director, Academic Achievement Program
University of Miami School of Law

Preface

Michael Serota

Law school has the potential to be one of the most rewarding experiences of your life, but it is an acquired taste. Many students find their first final exam period to be confusing, stressful, and filled with uncertainty. This book will teach you how to let the sunshine in. It delivers an easy-to-digest, methodological approach to writing successful law school exams, with Alex Schimel's characteristic enthusiasm, optimism, and realism.

Alex was my 1L study partner. We sensed early on that something was wrong with our approach to preparing for law school exams. Our professors were focusing on policy in class, but we discovered that law school exams were primarily about practical application of the law. The real wakeup call for me came when I received an F on a practice midterm. It was obvious that undergraduate "memorization tactics" were not going to cut it.

Alex and I took a big gamble. We teamed up and took responsibility for "learning the law" ourselves. Absolving our professors of all responsibility to prepare us for our final exams, we sought out other ways to learn. In the process, we inadvertently learned how to think like real lawyers, working backwards from problems to solutions, rather than blindly memorizing rules and cases.

The gamble paid off. Alex finished his first year of law school ranked number one in our class, and I finished second. Between the two of us, we earned only one grade below an A. That's because on the last exam of the entire year, I decided to conduct a personal experiment by writing an exam based on the professor's course outline, rather than on our methodology. Needless to say, it didn't work and I had to settle for a B+.

Finishing behind Alex was one of the greatest privileges of my academic career. I say that because Alex is one of the most compassionate, warm, friendly human beings I know. In all of our efforts at achieving personal success, we always sought out ways to bring other students along with us—first within our study groups, and then with Alex's free seminars at the law school. This book is the culmination of our desire to help guide others through the process that shaped us so thoroughly.

After our successful 1L year, we took different directions. I worked as the sole 1L summer associate at a top international firm, and then took a leave of absence from school to study ancient Jewish law in Jerusalem. Alex split his summers between public service work and a prestigious law firm in Miami. He finished school at UM (Summa Cum Laude, Order of the Coif) and is now at that same Miami firm full time. I ended up transferring to Berkeley Law School, and currently work as a federal law clerk in Washington, D.C.

In law school, you learn a lot about yourself. I learned the true meaning of hard work, perseverance, and the value of having an organized approach to exam taking. I also learned the importance of having a good friend with whom to prepare. First-year law school exams demand an incredible amount of dedication. You will answer difficult questions, based on a wide array of substantive material, in a very short period of time. Alex's book will help you develop the skills, strategy, and confidence necessary to succeed.

With that in mind, work hard, work smart, do your best, and be satisfied with the results, knowing that you did everything within your power to make your professional goals a reality. Take Alex's suggestions to heart, and make his methods your own. With training and preparation, you can make the law school exam-taking process a labor of love.

Law School Exams

Section I

Your Law School Experience Is About to Change

A. The Day of Epiphany

I remember the day pretty well. It was about six weeks into my first semester of law school. I was lying on the floor of my unfurnished apartment, staring up at the ceiling. I was smiling, but there were tiny teardrops forming at the corners of my eyes. I had been working non-stop for the last three days and I had barely put a scratch in my reading assignments. I wasn't going to finish in time for class. I wouldn't even come close.

I was laughing, but it wasn't funny. There was no way I could work this hard and accomplish so little. This was impossible. Law school was impossible. I had to quit.

When faced with a personal, professional, and emotional crisis, I did what any self-sufficient young adult does: I called my mom.

"I'm done, I'm coming home." I told her.

She probably said something reassuring or encouraging. Actually, I think she told me that she moved my bed into the garage and turned my room into a home office. I wasn't really listening—my head was buzzing from lack of sleep.

While she spoke, I tried to think of a believable rationalization for quitting law school and moving back home. Something that would convince my friends and family that I wasn't an ordinary failure; I was quitting on principle. "Law school is just another part of America's machine of corporate greed and corruption. It's about lies and deception, and I'm not going to be part of that system." That sounded pretty good.

Later that day, my friend and study partner Mike Serota picked me up, and we went for a drive around Miami. Mike is a dynamic person, with infectious enthusiasm and charm. We shared a mutual love and frustration with law school, and he was the perfect foil to my introverted and anxious personality.

"I think I had a nervous breakdown this afternoon," I told him.

He laughed, "Me too. Today was horrible. I barely finished half of the reading."

I felt better knowing that I wasn't the only one suffering. Mike was a hard worker. If he couldn't do it, I doubt anyone else could either. We decided that finished or not, he and I were finished for the day. We weren't even going to try to do any more work.

I didn't know it then, but it was the most important day of my law school career. It was the epiphany day. It was the day I realized that I was doing everything wrong. I was making law school much harder than it actually was. If I was going to succeed (and survive), I needed to make some serious changes.

Every law student has this epiphany moment. For some, it happens early, when they realize that the work is insurmountable. For others, it happens when they work extremely hard, only to receive a shockingly low exam grade. This is the turning point in a law student's life. This is where the road forks in two directions and you have to choose a path.

Most students respond to the epiphany by admitting defeat and resigning themselves to mediocre grades. "I worked hard and I still got a C. What's the point? Let's get a beer." Others realize that success is possible, but it will take more than just brute hard work. You need enthusiasm, a solid strategy, and a firm determination to beat the professors at their own game.

Mike and I sat down and made a whole new battle plan. Much less reading, much more sleep, and a singular focus on exams. If something wasn't going to be helpful for the exam, we ignored it. Learning the material in all five of our classes was way too ambitious. There was just too much to learn and not enough time. So we decided to learn just one thing instead: *How to take exams.*

There was one problem. We had never actually taken a law school exam. How do you prepare for something that you know nothing about? It was a big risk, and we knew it could backfire. Luckily for us, our plan worked perfectly. Mike and I both got straight *As* in our first semester of Law School. We finished our first year of Law School ranked number 1 and 2 in our class, with about half-a-dozen book awards between us.[1] We showed the strategy to other students, and it worked for them too. Mike and I had both heard a lot of "tips" and "advice" about law school before, and some of it was helpful. But now we had something really worthwhile: A strategy that we could actually *use.*

B. Getting in the Right Frame of Mind

Law School Is Mental

Right now, you are your own biggest obstacle to law school success. You have the potential to get *As*, but you are not reaching the depth of that ability, because your attention is divided in too many directions. This book will help you maximize your potential by boosting the only important skill you need—the ability to take law school exams. If your focus is elsewhere (excepting important things like family, health, and sleep), your performance will suffer. Surgeons prepare for surgery, lawyers prepare for trials, and law students prepare for exams. Maintaining this perspective will help you.

---

1. The "book" or "book award" is an accolade given by many law schools to the student in each class who earns the top grade on the exam. In the old days, winning the award earned you a free textbook (hence the name "book award"). Now, it's just an honor that appears on your transcript.

Law School Is Personal

Everyone approaches law school slightly differently, and there is no single magic-trick that guarantees universal success. Like any good advice, you will need to use your own judgment in applying the techniques you learn in this book. If a particular strategy doesn't make sense to you, or seems counterintuitive, I suggest that you just try it for a while. If you find that it doesn't suit your taste (after at least giving it a good test drive), you should drop it and try something else. Anyone who tells you that they have a 100% guaranteed, paint-by-number formula for writing an *A+* law school exam is lying. There are a thousand ways to write an *A+* exam and you need to figure out how *you* are going to do it.

So, Why Do You Need This Book?

Over the next hundred-or-so pages, you will learn a top-to-bottom strategy for approaching law school. In law school, you will meet some students who get *A*s by sheer talent. They read the books, listen in class, and then just write exams off the top of their heads. They get good grades, but they couldn't possibly teach you how to emulate their technique. Actually, they have no technique. They're just freaks of nature. You should wish them good luck, admire their natural genius, and ignore them completely. If you are like me, you need something that you can use; a concrete and practical methodology. This book offers real techniques that you can start using right away to improve your exam performance.

Breaking the "Rules"

Law school is unfair for many reasons. First of all, the academic curve means that your success is related to the performance of your peers. Second, there is no standardized method of examination—professors can test you however they choose, and can penalize you arbitrarily. Third, there's no handbook: You have to figure out the "rules" of the law school game as you play. If you're lucky, these "rules" start to become apparent around the second or third semester. But by that time, you've already taken about a dozen tests, probably with mixed results.

This book was developed with the support of Joanne Harvest Koren, director of the Academic Achievement Program at the University of Miami School of Law.[2] As a 2L, Joanne hired me to teach a two-hour workshop on exam skills. Over the following semesters, the workshop evolved into an eight-week comprehensive exam seminar for law students. With Joanne's encouragement, I have condensed the essential elements of that seminar into this book. These strategies have helped hundreds of students succeed in law school, and they are now in your hands. There is no "rule book" but this is as close as you can get.

C. A Note About Law School Grades

Grades Aren't Everything — Really

If you only focus on your GPA, you will miss many opportunities to learn, make friends, and start building your professional network. But good grades will really expand your career options when you graduate. Unfortunately, your first-year (1L) grades are much more important than your grades during the rest of law school. Many students who do poorly during their first year are able to work hard and get back on track before graduation. But you'll spend the rest of law school playing catch-up instead of launching out of the gate with a strong start. Additionally, if you plan to compete for a prestigious clerkship or summer associate position, your 1L grades will matter more than your graduating GPA. So grades aren't everything, but I'm not going to lie and say that they don't matter at all.

---

2. Joanne graciously wrote the foreword to this book and is a national expert in law school academic support. Her Academic Achievement Program at UM, which has helped thousands of law students succeed in law school, is recognized as one of the best academic support programs in the nation.

Re-adjust Your Internal Curve

You need to have a healthy relationship with grades. This starts by welcoming a new letter into your life—the *B*. In law school, a *B+* is a very high grade. You may be the type of person who feels like anything less than an *A* is a failure, but you simply cannot have that attitude in law school. *A*s are extremely difficult to obtain and most professors will only award nine or ten in a class of 150 students. Your future employers know this, and students with *B/B+* averages are taken very seriously. If you are getting more *C*s than *B*s then you have a problem and you need to make a change. But if you are a solid *B* student, you might not be doing as poorly as you think. So, relax a little.

The Two Key Elements of an A Exam

To get an *A* or a solid *B+*, you need to accomplish both of the following tasks:

- **Know the course material extremely thoroughly**
- **Write a clear, well-organized essay answer that is responsive to the question**

That may seem obvious, but accomplishing both tasks simultaneously is extremely difficult. Most students put too much emphasis on the first task, and neglect the second task. You absolutely need both to succeed.

D. Are You Reading This Book Too Late? Too Soon?

No matter where you are in your law school education, you should be striving to improve your exam performance. It's never too late, as long as you are willing to endure some discomfort as you overhaul your preparation techniques. You have no time to lose—your new approach must begin today.

However, if you are a 1L student, you shouldn't really start worrying about exam preparation until about the sixth week of the first semester. As a 1L, you need to develop your own natural rhythm for attending class, doing readings, and taking notes before you can add the stress of exam preparation.

E. The "Issue-Spotter Exam"

This book is about preparing for the typical issue-spotter essay exam, which is the most common form of law school testing. In an issue-spotter you will be given a hypothetical fact pattern (commonly referred to as the "hypo"), which will contain multiple legal issues. You pretend that you are an attorney representing one of the characters in the narrative, and your task is to prepare a "memo" on the legal claims that you identify.

What's a Memo?

I really wish that professors would stop using the word "memo" on their exams, because it confuses many students. You may have written memos for your legal writing class, or in your prior career. Whatever you think the word "memo" means — just forget it. In the context of law school exams, we are talking about something different. This kind of "memo" is a complex, highly analytical, and unique style of essay writing that has no other application outside of law school. When you see the "M" word in your exam booklet, mentally replace it with "issue-spotter exam answer."

In the real world, "memos" are cute little letters with fancy formatting that you write to your co-workers. In the exam world, issue-spotter answers are dirty, concise, no-frills essays that you write specifically for a professor. If you handed an exam answer into the managing partner at a law firm, she'd fire you. If you hand a typical "memo" to your professor, you'll get a C. Now that you've un-learned about memos, you'll spend the rest of this book re-learning about issue-spotter exam answers.

What Is NOT Being Tested on the Issue-Spotter

In a history class, you can earn a perfect exam score by accurately remembering every event, every character, and every date from the textbook and lectures. On a law school exam, remembering everything from your casebook and class lectures will earn you a big zero.

You are not being tested on your knowledge of the "law" or the contents of your book. Your professor is simply not impressed if you remember all of the elements of negligence or equitable servitudes (or whatever else you were supposed to be learning). By the time the exam rolls around, professors expect you to have a thorough understanding of every concept presented in the lectures and readings. If you *don't* know a particular concept, that will be a problem. But merely knowing all the cases and rules won't get you very far.

What IS Being Tested

Let's identify the main things your professor is looking for when she is grading exams:

- Your ability to read a fact pattern and identify the potential legal claims, defenses, and related issues.
- Your ability to apply your knowledge of the law to those facts.
- Your ability to make clear and well-reasoned arguments about the legal issues you have identified.
- Your ability to see the issues from multiple perspectives; realistically evaluating the strengths and weaknesses of your assertions and arguments.
- Your ability to organize your thoughts, arguments, and analysis into a cogent and easy-to-read essay, within the time allotted.

Professors approach this exam format in a variety of ways, and may differ in how they weigh the individual grading criteria. For example, some professors will reward you for creative thinking and problem solving, while others will penalize you for it. Despite these variables, there are specific skills and writing techniques that will satisfy even the most discriminating grader.

Other Types of Questions or Exam Formats

The typical law school exam has two or more issue-spotter essays, but may also include other types of questions (e.g., multiple choice, true-false, policy essays, etc.) There are also professors who administer entire exams in multiple choice format, take-home exams, or offer research papers instead of tests. Generally speaking, you already have the basic skills to handle every kind of law school exam format *except* the issue-spotter. For most other formats, your substantive knowledge of the material is all that is required. If you have questions about preparing for a different exam format, your best bet is to ask the professor directly.

Section II

Preparation for Exam Writing

My study partner Mike and I got together every Sunday to practice writing exam answers. We would find an empty classroom at the law school, and spend a few hours debating, strategizing, and writing. Our first goal was to identify the essential elements of an A+ exam. What were professors really looking for? Was this an art or a science? If it was more scientific than creative (which we believed), our next goal was to create a template that hit all the essential elements, and could be replicated on every exam. Each of our courses was very different, and the professors had distinct perspectives, tendencies, and demands. But learning how to please each one of them individually seemed impossible. Instead, our plan was to draw them all into our box; find a single structure that was good enough to apply to any exam.

This was an ambitious task, especially because we had no idea what we were doing, and we had never actually taken a law school exam. We would spread all of our books, supplements, and outlines on the desks — open to various chapters, because we couldn't remember anything from class. We wasted a lot of time looking things up, but it was unavoidable. We both had lousy memories and short attention spans.

We wrote collaboratively; dictating our answers out-loud, taking turns typing or writing on the board. Our early attempts were simply awful. The essays were overly formulaic, way too long, and took between three to six hours to complete. But Sunday after Sunday, we kept working, until finally we wrote something good. It was a Torts essay, it took an hour and fifteen minutes to write, and I felt like framing it. It was really good.

"How do we know that it's good?" asked Mike. "We've never taken a real test. Maybe they are expecting something else."

"It's good." I said. "It has to be good. It's got everything. It's organized, it's concise, and it covers all aspects of the question. It's good, I'm positive."

"Yeah." said Mike. "You're right. It's good."

I slouched down in my chair, exhausted. "Man, how did they expect us to figure that out on our own?"

A. The Basics: Understanding Black Letter Law

Starting from Scratch

Before you can write an exam, you've got to know what you're writing about. You're not writing about Torts, Property, or Civil Procedure; you're writing about the application of rules to factual scenarios. What rules? Well, there are a lot of them, and you will have to learn them all. But before you start making flashcards, it's helpful to take a step back and examine the nature of these rules. As you demystify "the law," you'll start to realize that these rules are manageable, practical, and useful. They are the fuel that you will use in your analysis. Merely memorizing them gets you nowhere, and is a lot more difficult than the strategy that I am about to propose.

We'll start by exploring how to write exam answers using bare abstract legal principles—so-called "black letter" rules. Later, we'll introduce another level of depth by using actual case holdings. If you're encountering a lot of statutory law in your courses, the technique is basically the same, so don't worry. Fortunately, most 1L courses (with the exception of Civil Procedure) don't really involve statutory analysis, so it's not a big obstacle.

What Is "Black Letter" Law?

You have probably heard the phrase "black letter" law, and you might be confused about its meaning. Generally when people talk about black letter law, they are referring to an abstract and absolute legal "rule" that distills the essential meaning out of a single case, or a series of cases. For example, if you asked a legally educated person for the black letter rule on common law larceny, she would say something like, "Common law larceny is the taking and carrying away of another person's property, with the intent to steal." Most lawyers, hornbooks, and judges would agree that this is the essential black letter rule on larceny. It is the law, stated in the abstract, apart from any particular context.

The Professor's View: "Black Letter Law Does Not Exist"

Many professors insist that there is no such thing as black letter law in a "common law" legal system (like America). Every case must be examined on its particular facts, and the holding from a specific decision is applicable only to the individual litigants involved. There are no absolute and abstract "rules." The doctrine of *stare decisis* (which you are probably sick of hearing about) means that a future case with similar facts should also have a similar holding. But nothing absolute or universal can be drawn from an individual decision; the analysis is always case-by-case, fact-by-fact.

In other words, if you want to know the "rule" for larceny, you need to go back and read a case from 1642 where a man carried away another man's goat and was found guilty of a common law crime (*see His Lordship Fardingwarls v. Bigsby Goatsmuggler*, 11 KBH 516 (1614)).[1] Then you need to evaluate whether the doctrine of *stare decisis* compels a similar decision in the present case. A one-line statement of any "rule" is inaccurate, because it is an over-generalization, which ignores the nuances of fact involved.

---

1. This is not a real case. Please don't cite to it on an exam.

The Law Student's View: "Just Give Me the Rule"

On the other hand, many law students are constantly trying to extract black letter rules from their cases and supplements. Their goal is to boil the entire casebook down to a series of *haiku* poems that they can fit onto a single flash card and then memorize. When the professor begins his *beauty of the common law* lecture for the sixteenth time, this student is thinking to himself, "Don't tell me about goats. Tell me about the law. Give me the rule and move on!" This student believes that with a series of simple, one-line rules, he will be able to answer any exam question.

The Truth: They're Both Right, and Both Wrong

In the real world of litigation, your professor is absolutely right. There are no fixed and simple rules that can be easily stated in a single sentence. When you are in front of an actual judge, you will need to show her complete case holdings, explain factual scenarios, and argue how they favor your position. **But for the purposes of law school exams, there is such a thing as black letter law. It is just not what you are thinking of.**

Most law school exam questions do not have a straight answer that can be cleanly and completely stated, like my rule for common law larceny. You need more flexibility in your understanding of the law, and factual analysis is critical. Think of the "rule" as a much larger principle, spread out over something that I call the **rings of analysis.** This is a framework of legal concepts that interconnect to form a more complete and multi-dimensional picture of the rule. It is somewhere in-between the two opposing views of our professor and student above. To please the student, it is an abstraction of the cases and doctrines, stated in singular and absolute terms. To please the professor, it is nuanced and flexible, rather than oversimplified and fixed.

If you understand how this works, it is possible to write exam answers without citing to a single case.

The Rings of Analysis

Your target is not to hit the "right answer" but rather to hit the "right framework." A one-line definitional answer is worth almost nothing. You will earn points by presenting a well-rounded analysis that approaches the fact pattern from several angles. By broadening your concept of the "rule" you increase your opportunity to earn points. You'll see why I call them "rings" in a few pages. For now, just bear with me.

Constructing the Rings

Somewhere in your studies, you may have picked up a one-line rule statement that has stuck in your memory. For example, "Assault is the intentional unlawful threat of force, causing apprehension of imminent bodily harm." That's a great little definition, and it's not incorrect. But it's worth very little on an exam. There is so much more to know about assault, and probably much more to discuss in your essay. In fact, there are maybe ten other black letter principles that you have learned about assault, and they must all be incorporated into your rings of analysis, in order to have a complete picture. For example, try jotting out a quick list of things you know about assault:

Example: Rings of Analysis on 'Assault'

- **Basic definition (also called the "cause of action" or "prima facie case"):** "Assault is the intentional, unlawful, threat of force, causing apprehension of imminent bodily harm."
- **Affirmative defenses:** Consent, necessity, self-defense, insanity, and involuntary bodily movement are all defenses to the tort (or crime) of assault.
- **Frequent issues:** "Words alone are not assault. Overt bodily movement is generally required"; "Apprehension requires knowledge of the threat, but not fear."
- **Potential defects in facts:** "Apprehension caused lawfully is not assault" (e.g., a police search); "A threat that is not imminent is not assault" (e.g., a threat made over the telephone).

A good answer will include some or all of these elements. They are all part of the "rule" on assault. It is possible to construct a network of rings like this for almost every topic in law school.

The Fourth Grade Science Fair Approach

One way to think of the rings of analysis is by picturing your Torts class as a fourth-grade model of the solar system. In the center is a giant yellow beach ball sun that says "Torts" on it. All topics related to the class must revolve around this sun, and only topics presented in your readings or class are allowed in the solar system. You have been given a limited set of information in your classes, and the professor is restricted to testing you on that material *only*.

Surrounding the sun are concentric rings of papier-mâché planets that say things like "intentional torts," "negligence," "strict liability," and "products liability." These are the major topic headings, or categories of subjects in your Torts class. They orbit around the center of your course.

Revolving around these planets are miniature tennis-ball moons displaying various sub-topics associated with each major topic. For example, planet "intentional torts" is surrounded by the moons "assault," "battery," "trespass," "conversion," and "defamation."

Each of these moons is then surrounded by smaller satellites (grapes, perhaps?) which represent the individual elements of each sub-topic. For example, on page 17 above, we listed various issues associated with the tort of assault. Each one of these points is like a tiny satellite revolving around the moon "assault."

I don't advise you to make an actual diorama (hey, that'd be fun though, wouldn't it?), but thinking of your classes in this way may help you stay focused when you study for exams. There isn't actually that much material in each class. Just a bunch of rules, related to a handful of topics, and it all fits into a nice cohesive framework. The trick is to put the solar system together in the right order—don't put your *products liability* "moons" around your *negligence* "planet."

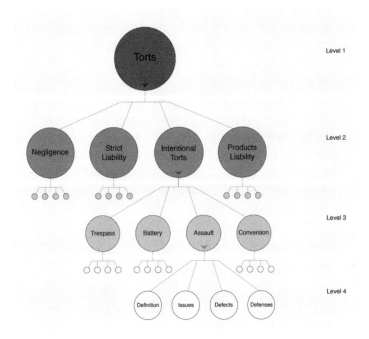

When you're analyzing a particular fact pattern on an exam, just aim for the right planet and navigate the moons. For example, on an exam question about the tort of assault, first head over to planet "intentional torts," then shoot over to the moon "assault." Pick out the two or three satellite issues that are relevant to the particular facts presented, and discuss why they may affect the outcome. That's all you have to do. It's as easy as ... well, rocket science.

Collect the Right Elements for Your Rings

How do you know what belongs in the solar system, and what is just random debris floating in space? There's no single source to rely on, but commercial outlines are a great place to start. These useful supplements will do much of the organization for you, by breaking the course into topics and sub-topics. They will also help you take a step back from the details of your cases and enter the world of black letter rules. There are several brands available, and choosing is a matter of sheer taste. Ask around to see which ones are good for your various classes and professors.

The holdings from cases are also an important source of material for the rings. Most likely, you will see factual scenarios on your exam that are similar to cases that you read in class. Case holdings add important nuance and dimension to your understanding of the topic. You can often reduce the case holdings to a simple abstract statement, as long as you recognize that they are just tiny satellites orbiting around a complex topic. They are a part of the rule, not the rule itself.

B. The Method: Introducing IRAHNC

IRAHNC Is the Most Important Practical Technique in This Book — Use It Wisely

If there is one concrete strategy that is going to improve your exam performance, this is it. No matter who you are or where you go to school, IRAHNC will help you write better exam answers. It is a simple, clean, and well-organized exam writing style that anyone can use. IRAHNC is by no means revolutionary; most top law students use it already, whether they realize it or not. But if nobody tells you about it, you probably won't figure it out on your own until it's too late.

Everything You Know about IRAC Is Wrong

The first four letters of this technique may look familiar. Everyone knows about IRAC ("Issue, Rule, Analysis, Conclusion"). It is the legal writing technique that is taught at most law schools, and it is so old and unpopular that it's basically a joke. Most students resist the IRAC method, especially on exams, for an obvious reason: *It doesn't work!*

The Critical Missing Piece: Counter-Arguments

Whoever invented IRAC (or its low-class cousin, CRAC) made a huge and unforgivable mistake. He left no room in the formula for counter-arguments, which are by far the most important part of any legal analysis. If you do not present the counter-arguments of your hypothetical opponent, your analysis is incomplete. In fact, it is so incomplete that it barely even qualifies as a responsive essay. Most professors will give you only minimal credit for an exam answer that fails to delve into the counter-arguments.

IRAHNC to the Rescue

Let's add two measly words to the IRAC formula and see what changes.

(I)ssue
(R)ule
(A)nalysis
(H)owever
(N)evertheless
(C)onclusion

The acronym is harder to pronounce, and there is no foreign country of the same name to help you remember it. But it works and IRAC doesn't, so use it.

"However-ing"

In the "However" portion of your essay, you present a counter-argument. You've made your argument (IRA), but now the opposing team gets to have their say. This imaginary opposing attorney is ready to defend against your argument, and he's got a few issues to raise himself.

Don't be afraid of the counter-arguments. If you want to perform a complete legal analysis, you need to show the defects in your own argument—what are the weaknesses that opposing counsel might exploit? Where are the gaps in your reasoning? Are there any other cases or doctrines that undermine your position? Get them out in the open now and show the professor that you are prepared to handle them.

"Nevertheless-ing"

Uh-oh! The other side actually has some pretty valid points. Your analysis in IRA turned out to be weaker than it seemed at first. So now what do you do? Run and hide? No! In the "Nevertheless" portion of your essay, you *rebut* the counter-arguments and re-assert your position. Maybe the argument from the other side is flawed. Maybe there is another rule or exception that saves the day. Your rebuttal might be weak, or legally tenuous, but at least you saw the counter-attack coming and you had something prepared to defend yourself.

Write Where the Points Are!

When your professor is grading exams, she's looking for counter-arguments and rebuttals. That's where you will pick up the major points.

A frequent complaint from professors is that students write in a "conclusory" manner. That's law professor code for, "You didn't include any counter-arguments and rebuttals." They expect to see this one-two-three punch combination—argument, counter-argument, rebuttal. It is absolutely required. IRAHNC covers all the bases in an organized and methodical way. It's as close as you can get to a "sure-fire" trick.

Get into the Right Frame of Mind

Why does IRAHNC work? Well, because issue-spotter exams are weird. You need to put yourself in a particular mindset in order to answer them correctly.

When you are writing, try to imagine a nerdy, obsessive-compulsive litigator who hates surprises. All she cares about is avoiding a sneak attack from opposing counsel. She picks and prods all of her arguments for weaknesses and flaws, just to make sure that she is aware of them ahead of time. If her opponent has a powerful counter-argument, she wants to know about it before he does. She doesn't care if she wins or loses; she just wants to have a thorough preview of all the potential arguments before stepping into court.

When you write an issue-spotter answer, you are looking at a fact scenario and imagining what will happen if litigation ensues. What is the plaintiff going to say? How will the defendant respond? How will the plaintiff rebut? That's as far as you have to go. Your goal is not to explain what *will happen*; that's impossible to predict (and your professor will penalize you for trying). Instead, just be satisfied to explain what *will be argued*. Then objectively evaluate these arguments and discuss their relative strengths. There's no need to draw a firm conclusion.

You Are NOT an Advocate

Unless the instructions explicitly instruct you to *advocate* for your client to win, you should not necessarily take the position that your client will win. Maybe he will win, maybe he won't—be objective and realistic, even though you are supposedly his attorney. Remember, you are that risk-averse, nerdy lawyer: All she cares about is being prepared, but she knows that she might not win.

An Example of IRAHNC in Action

Here's a short, simple hypothetical in the subject of Torts. We'll use it to take a test drive of the IRAHNC format:

> Drake was standing on the balcony of his second floor apartment. He looked down at Paul who was walking below in the parking lot. Drake yelled to Paul, "When I see you at the convention next Tuesday, I'm going to punch your lights out." As Drake yelled, he held a broomstick over his head. Paul felt scared and ran away. You are Paul's attorney. Prepare a memo on the likely outcome of the case.

First, Get Oriented by Doing Some Quick Issue-spotting

The facts strongly suggest that our analysis should focus on the tort of assault. How do we spot that? Run through the different major and minor topics in the subject of Torts (i.e., the "planets" and "moons" in our solar system model). Check which topics relate to the facts.

We can quickly eliminate negligence, products liability, and strict liability, based on the facts. We're somewhere within the intentional torts arena. You might have thought of intentional infliction of emotional distress, but simple fear is usually not enough to support that claim. You might have also thought of some of the defamatory or privacy torts, but those are also off target (you can just trust me on that, or look it up).

This is definitely an assault question. If you didn't spot that, don't worry, you'll sharpen your skills as you go.

Flip back to page 17 for the "rings of analysis" on the tort of assault. A few issues jump out in this hypo:

- **Drake's act might not constitute an assault, because it was "mere words":** The tort of assault requires more than just threatening verbal statements—an overt bodily movement is also necessary. Drake made a movement, but was it part of the threat? Do Drake's bodily gestures satisfy this requirement?

- **Drake's threat may not have been sufficiently imminent to qualify as an assault:** In order for a threat to constitute an assault, it must create an "imminent apprehension of bodily harm." Was Drake's threat to harm Peter on a future occasion sufficient?

We don't have to answer these questions. It's enough to identify that they are present in the hypothetical.

Next, Let's See What an IRAHNC Essay Would Look Like with These Issues in Mind

I've broken the essay into its elements and added headings for clarity. Obviously, don't write the headings "Issue, Rule, Analysis, etc." on a real exam. Ordinary paragraphs will suffice.

Issue: Paul may wish to bring an assault claim against Drake.

Rule: Assault is defined as an intentional act that causes reasonable apprehension of harmful or offensive contact, coupled with the imminent ability to execute such contact.

Analysis: Here, Drake verbally threatened to attack Paul. Paul appears to have experienced apprehension of harmful contact, as demonstrated by his fearful flight from the area. Therefore, Drake may be liable for the tort of assault.

However #1 (words alone): However, Drake may counter-argue that mere verbal threats are not sufficient to constitute an assault—some overt bodily movement is required. Drake will claim that his threat was verbal, and therefore not an assault.

Nevertheless #1: Nevertheless, Drake's verbal threat was coupled with his act of holding a broom over his head. Unless there was another reason why Drake had the broom in the air, it seems possible that this posture was part of the threat, or meant to create apprehension of harm in Paul. Thus, a court may find that this action was more than just mere words.

However #2 (lack of imminence): Drake may further counter-argue that, even if his act was more than mere words, his threat was not sufficiently imminent to constitute an assault. First, Drake was standing high up on a balcony and probably could not execute his threat immediately. Second, Drake said he was going to punch Paul "next Tuesday" which may not be sufficiently imminent to constitute an assault.

Nevertheless #2: Nevertheless, Paul may argue that Drake could have easily thrown the broomstick that he was holding, and his posture suggested that he might do so imminently. This fact, coupled with Drake's apparently aggressive demeanor and hostile statements may have demonstrated an imminent ability to inflict harm.

Conclusion: Paul may have a cause of action for assault, but there are significant defects and credible defenses. This claim is worth pursuing, but it might not prevail.

Breakdown of the Essay Format

Issue: In the "issue" line, all you want to do is indicate to the professor that you've spotted the right legal issue. You're not saying that this claim has any merit; you're just saying that it's *possible* that this person *might consider* bringing this type of claim, based on the facts you were given.

Rule: Notice that I've stated the rule in the abstract. A simple one-line statement will usually suffice here. I've just dropped in the definition from our rings of analysis. Most often the definition is the launch pad for your first argument.

Analysis: Now I compare the facts of the hypo to the rule from my rings. I try to incorporate some of the buzzwords from the definition. In a traditional (i.e., lousy) IRAC essay, you would probably cram a lot more discussion into this analysis section, and you might ramble on for a whole page without moving on to the next part. But if you discussed everything here, you'd have nothing left to present in the form of counter-arguments and re-buttals later on. So I leave some big issues unstated. My essay will be much more interesting to a professor if it is framed as a *debate* rather than just an explanation. Point, counterpoint, rebuttal — like real litigation.

I end my analysis with a "soft" conclusion: "Therefore, Drake may be liable for the tort of assault." This acts like a pause in the argument structure. It says to the professor, "I've now set up my skeleton argument and I'm going to test its strength by attacking it from various angles." Notice that my conclusion is very non-committal: "Drake *may* be liable . . ." That's hardly saying anything at all, and that's about as strong as you should be at this point.

However #1: Now I test the strength of my proposition by raising a counter-argument. I draw something else out of the rings of analysis that seems to contradict the soft conclusion. A "mere words" argument is not very compelling in this case, but it's not totally without merit either. If Drake was actually in court, his attorney would almost certainly try to argue it. So as Paul's over-prepared, risk-averse attorney, I have to tackle it.

Nevertheless #1: Now all I do is point out the factual defect in Drake's assertion. There *was* a bodily movement, and circumstances suggest that it was part of the threat. Is this sufficient to satisfy the requirement? I have no idea, and I don't care. I don't need to decide who will win this argument. I set up a proposition, he makes a counter-argument, and then I make a rebuttal. That's as far as you have to go with this kind of essay.

However #2: I have more than one counter-argument to raise. Rather than lump them all together, I just repeat the cycle a few times. So my essay actually proceeds in the structure of IRAHNHNC. The acronym is harder to pronounce, but the essay will be much easier for the professor to read.

In my second counter-argument, I argue that Drake's action doesn't actually fit the definition of assault: The requirement of imminence may be lacking. I point to two facts that support this counter-assertion: Drake's statement and his physical distance from Paul. These are both potent arguments, and it's pretty clear from the hypothetical that the professor wants me to address them.

Nevertheless #2: Now I've got a problem, because Drake's second counter-argument (However #2) is very damaging to my assault claim. Drake might be correct; his threat may not have been sufficiently imminent to constitute a legally cognizable assault. I have two choices at this point, both of which are acceptable: First, I can concede that Drake's counter-argument is too powerful to rebut and just admit that I have no real defense. Alternatively, I can try to come up with a *reasonable* rebuttal, even if it is not very strong. I opted for the latter choice—a weak argument that Drake could have thrown his broom. It's a bit of a stretch, but it works.

Conclusion: At this point in the essay, I take a step backwards and look at the big picture—is this claim a total loser, or can I remedy its defects with credible arguments? My response is non-committal, objective, and conservative. I end almost every IRAHNC essay with some variation of this sentence: "[Client] may have a cause of action for [whatever] against [Defendant], but there are significant defects. This claim is [probably/probably not] worth pursuing."

Conclusions Are Worthless

Here's the big joke: *It doesn't matter what you say in your conclusion.* The conclusion is worth practically nothing on the professor's score sheet. This is totally contradictory to everything you know about academic testing. On a math or chemistry exam, you might get partial credit for showing your analysis, but the conclusion is what matters most. On a law school exam, your ability to identify issues and make arguments is 100% of your score. Whether you think the client will win or lose is usually irrelevant.

Your professor probably doesn't even know who should win, and she intentionally wrote the hypothetical to make it unclear. If you take all of the top-scoring exam answers in a class, 50% of them will say Drake wins, and 50% will say Paul wins. It doesn't matter which side you choose, as long as you present a balanced and thorough analysis that is responsive to the hypothetical.

Hypos with Multiple Issues

This hypo was fairly simple because there was only one issue to address. Most hypotheticals on an actual exam will have multiple issues related to the same fact pattern—perhaps an assault, a battery, some negligence issues, etc. I have heard of students who adhere so strictly to the IRAC format, that they attempt to cram all of it into a gigantic one-paragraph essay. That's a big mistake. One round of IRAHNC should cover one issue only. Your essay should contain as many repetitions of the IRAHNC formula as is necessary to address all of the issues.

Advice about Issue Spotting

When you are issue spotting, pay close attention to the facts. Professors rarely include facts that aren completely irrelevant to your analysis.[2] So you should constantly be asking yourself, "Why did the professor include that particular fact?" Why was Drake on the second floor balcony instead of the first floor? Why did he have a broom? These facts were included to provide you with ammunition for your arguments and they should be addressed in your essay.

If the hypo says, "John was wearing a red sweater," spend a moment really picking that apart. Why bother saying that the sweater was red? Does it make him more visible in a crowd or easier for a witness to identify? Why say anything about his clothes at all? Does his sweater suggest that he was intentionally prepared for cold weather? Don't go crazy over-analyzing every single word, but pay attention to these kinds of details, because they often matter.

"My Professor Specifically Warned Us to Avoid IRAC on His Exam, and This Looks Too Similar. What Do I Do?"

Use IRAHNC anyway. When a professor tells you not to use IRAC, he's doing so because of his personal aversion to that writing style. If he made a point of warning you about it in class, he's very nit-picky and he's probably going to be a hard grader. But there is simply no way to write a well-rounded and fully developed essay without at least using the *elements* of IRAHNC. You have to identify issues, you have to know the rule, you have to analyze the issues, and you need to present counter-arguments. I used IRAHNC on every essay exam, no matter what the professor said, and it always worked.

When a professor says "Don't write with IRAC" you have to interpret that statement. They probably mean one of two things:

---

2. But it does happen. See page 64 for a discussion of "red herring" fact patterns—misleading facts that look like real issues, but are actually distracters.

First, they may be saying, "Don't write out a long explanation of the rules; just get to your arguments." In this case, just reduce or omit your statement of the rule. Try using "IAHNC" instead. As long as you don't skimp on the remaining categories, the method still works.

Second, your professor may be saying, "Don't be so formulaic in your writing style; give me something insightful and personal." In that case, write with IRAHNC anyway, despite their warning. Your professor is too picky and peculiar and you'll never be able to guess what they are looking for. These professors are the most challenging, and you'll go insane trying to guess their intention. Your best bet is to do a solid IRAHNC essay and let them deduct points for style. If you blow them away with a very thorough analysis, you'll probably still get a top grade.

Scared about Using IRAHNC? Take It to the Source

Get one of your professor's old exams or a generic hypothetical and write a practice essay using IRAHNC. Then schedule an office visit with your professor, hand him the essay, and ask for feedback. The vast majority of professors will happily review your practice exam and give you tons of valuable advice about where you went wrong. You'll know exactly what to do, and whether IRAHNC will work in that class.

Why doesn't everyone do this? I have no idea. Maybe they don't want good grades.

C. Cases as Authority in an IRAHNC Essay

Introducing Case Law into the Formula

In the first part of this section, we looked at an essay answer that presented a complete, well-rounded response to a hypothetical without citing any cases. We used our black letter rings of analysis, and just plugged in the different aspects of our "rule."

On many exams, this will suffice. Many professors don't care whether you cite cases or not.

However, in some classes (and with some professors), directly citing to cases is unavoidable. You need to discuss the cases that you read and use them dynamically in your essay. It sounds a lot harder than what we've done so far, but it's not. It's just a tiny twist on the IRAHNC format. Once you master this small maneuver, you're on fire. Your essays will really jump out of the grading pile.

The "There/Here" Method

When you write an essay with cases, you are trying to accomplish a very specific goal. You want to show that a case from your syllabus may affect the outcome of the hypothetical. More specifically, you're trying to compare the <u>facts</u> from the case to the <u>facts</u> of the hypo, and then predict the outcome. If the facts are sufficiently similar, you'll argue that the outcome should be the same. If the facts are sufficiently different, you'll argue that the outcome should not be the same.

The Power Switch

The words "there" and "here" have magical significance in legal writing. They function like a directional switch in the mind of your reader. When writing with cases, you need to make complex comparative arguments (i.e., comparing *this thing* to *that thing*). The words "there" and "here" allow you to move back and forth between concepts, without too much confusion or intricate wordplay. Here's a very simple (and sad) example.

We are evaluating the health of Bradley the dog. A scientist determined that all dogs with the Z gene will get stomach cancer by the age of 7. <u>There</u>, the scientist determined that all Poofle dogs have the Z gene. <u>Here</u>, we have Bradley, a 5-year-old Poofle dog who does not have stomach cancer. Based on this, we can conclude that Bradley will get stomach cancer within the next two years.

We have two subjects in this paragraph—Bradley's health, and the scientist's research. Bradley's health is my primary subject; it is the topic of my essay. The scientist's research is a secondary subject; something that is relevant to analyzing my topic, but is not the topic itself.

When I say "there," it tells the reader: "This is what happened *over there*, at that scientist's laboratory." It was a different time, and a different place.

When I say, "here," it tells the reader: "Now we're talking about what's going on *over here*, with Bradley the dog." The word "here" always refers to the primary subject of our essay segment.

When we are working with cases, we do the same thing: "There" means what happened *over there*, in that other case at another time. "Here" means what happened *over here*, with the characters this hypo. If it doesn't make sense yet, that's ok. We'll work through it again.

Integrating Cases into IRAHNC

We use the "There/Here" method to make a comparison between one of our cases and the facts in our hypothetical. To do this, we need to make a little more breathing room in the IRAHNC format. We break the "Rule" section into three parts, and we break the "Analysis" section into two parts. We end up with IRRRAAHNC.

An Example of the "There/Here" Method in Action

Issue: Raise your issue (the topic): In order to succeed in his assault claim, Paul must prove that Drake's actions constituted an imminent threat of bodily harm.

Rule (1): Introduce your case: The court evaluated a similar situation in ASTRO v. BARKLEY.

Rule (2): Discuss the facts of that case: *There*, the defendant made verbal threats and waved his arms in an enraged manner, while advancing on foot towards the plaintiff from several yards away.

Rule (3): Give the rule of law from that case: The court in ASTRO held that verbal threats accompanied by physically aggressive body movements demonstrate an imminent threat of bodily harm, even when made from a distance.

Analysis (1): List the facts from the hypo that are similar to the facts in the case: *Here*, Drake shouted a threat at Peter from an second floor balcony and held a broomstick over his head.

Analysis (2): Explain the similarity between these two situations: A court may find that the combination of verbal threats and aggressive arm movements in ASTRO are similar to Drake's verbal threats and actions with the broomstick. In both situations, the words and bodily gestures seemed to demonstrate intent to inflict harm, even though made from a distance. Therefore, a court may determine that Drake's actions created an imminent threat of bodily harm.

However: However, Drake may argue that the present situation can be distinguished from ASTRO. *There*, the defendant was advancing on foot towards the plaintiff. *Here*, Drake was standing on a second floor balcony, and remained at the same distance from Paul during the entire incident. Since it was impossible for Drake to advance towards Paul, a court may find that these situations are too dissimilar. Therefore, a court may decide not to follow the decision in ASTRO, and not to find Drake's threat sufficiently imminent.

Nevertheless: Nevertheless, Paul may argue the facts *here* are sufficiently similar to ASTRO, despite Drake's argument. *Here*, Drake was holding a broomstick, which he could have used as a projectile. Thus, Drake had the potential to inflict immediate physical harm, even though he was far away. Therefore, Paul can argue that ASTRO is still controlling, because Drake's ability to advance was irrelevant to his ability to inflict imminent harm.

Conclusion: ASTRO is not directly on point, but it may be helpful to Paul's claim, provided that the judge is not persuaded by Drake's argument for distinction. This claim is worth pursuing, but it has significant defects.

Breakdown of the Essay Format

In the first six sections, we simply expanded the IRA portion to make room for our comparative analysis. We use "there" and "here" to switch back and forth between our two subjects (the ASTRO case, and our facts from the hypo).

Take a look at the However section. It's just condensed version of the first three steps (IRRRAA), but we argue how the case is *dissimilar* instead of how it is similar. Then in Nevertheless, we bolster our original position in the same way. Notice that it's not always necessary to write out the whole formula: Sometimes you can fit multiple parts into a single sentence, or leave out parts altogether. With practice, you will gain flexibility, and you'll start to do this naturally. For now, stick to the format.

Ditch The Bluebook

Forget the *Bluebook* style when you are writing essays. The only thing that matters when citing to cases is clarity — the professor needs to know exactly which case you are talking about. I liked to use all capital letters whenever I referred to a case by name, but you could use boldface, underline, stars, etc. Just pick a system and be consistent throughout the essay. Typically, I would do something like this: "A manager is liable for the torts of his employees (OWENS v. BURGER)." Or alternatively, "As the court established in the case OWENS, managers are liable for the torts of their employees." Leave out the year, the reporter, and all that other junk. Occasionally, if you are citing a Supreme Court opinion, it *may* be helpful to know the author of the opinion in order to distinguish it from the dissents.

Ditch the Case Name

If you can't remember the name of a particular case, you can still cite to it. Just pick out one of the very memorable facts and cite to it as, "The case where the monkey burned down a library." Your professor will know exactly what you are talking about, and probably won't penalize you for failing to remember the name of the case. Of course if you can remember case names, it is a little easier for you and your professor.

Quick Case References

You don't always need to use "There/Here" method when you want to reference a case. Some case holdings are strong enough to stand on their own, even without referencing the facts. For example, "A religious marriage does not create a legal contract unless a marriage certificate is filed in the county records (HALBERT)." There might not be anything more to say on the matter, in which case you just treat it like a "black letter" rule and do a normal IRAHNC analysis.

Section III

Taking the Actual Exam

Up until now, we've discussed various techniques for improving your exam preparation skills. Now we turn to the dynamics of the exam itself. The proctor will say "Pencils up," and four hours later "Pencils down." What should you do in between?

A. The Four Requirements for a Great Exam

All good exam writers tackle these four essential requirements, although they may not do so in a methodical manner. These elements are all interrelated, but they also involve distinct skill sets. First we'll walk through the four requirements generally, and then we will identify a four-step process for accomplishing each in turn:

- **Requirement 1: Understanding the hypo:** You must understand the hypo in a thorough manner, paying close attention to details. If you fail to understand the issues, overlook important facts, or simply misread portions of the text, you are giving away points unnecessarily.

- **Requirement 2: Issue spotting:** Identify the operative legal issues, arguments, and counter-arguments in the hypo. Which facts create legal claims and defenses? Which facts support or contradict your principal arguments? Which facts are suggestive of cases or rules from your course? You must pull out the important issues that will form the basis of your essay.

- **Requirement 3: Organized analysis:** Analyze the legal issues with a logical and well-organized structure. Certain fundamental issues or topics should be analyzed before delving into ancillary issues or defenses. Your essay should have a predictable rhythm and be framed as a point-counterpoint debate.

- **Requirement 4: Clear presentation:** Write a clear and comprehensive essay that demonstrates your ability to accomplish tasks 1 through 3.

B. Satisfying the Four Requirements

The Naturals

Some students with strong reading comprehension skills and great proficiency with essay writing may be able to satisfy all four of these requirements instinctively and simultaneously. They have a high capacity for mental multi-tasking and can meet these distinct challenges automatically. Like a great chess player, they can see many moves ahead without obvious strain or calculation.

Everyone Else

Most students, however, would benefit from attacking these requirements one at a time. Satisfy requirement 1 and then move on to number 2. By focusing on only one goal at a time, you stay organized throughout the process.

Third, Flip Through the Entire Exam and Pick a Question

Get a sense of how many questions there are on the exam and what question formats you'll be dealing with. On most exams, you won't be forced to answer the questions in any particular order. I recommend tackling the hard-looking questions first. Whatever you do, don't dwell at this stage for too long; after a few moments of browsing, you should just pick a question and get started.

Once You've Picked, Go Straight to the Hypo Instruction Paragraph

Before you read a hypo, drop down to the bottom of the page. Usually, there will be an instruction paragraph that looks something like this:

> "You are a junior associate at Bing, Ding, & Ring LLP. Peter has come to your office to ask about a possible lawsuit. Assume the laws of State X apply to this case. Please prepare a memo discussing the merits of his potential claims."

Without even reading the hypo, this paragraph has told you a lot of important information:

1) **There's somebody named Peter in this hypo, and you are his lawyer.** That means all of the issues you will write about must involve Peter in some way. As you are reading, you can basically ignore any issues that don't involve him.

- **Potential twists:** Instead of being an attorney, the instructions might tell you to be a judge, a clerk, or a legislative aid proposing a new law. While these may seem like more difficult scenarios, with practice you will see that it doesn't make much difference what role you are instructed to play. You just move through the same arguments, counter-arguments, and rebuttals regardless of who you are supposed to be. Remember, this is all about objective analysis, not argumentative advocacy. Don't believe me? Try re-writing one of your previous practice exams from the perspective of another player. It will be almost exactly the same.

2) **The law of State X applies in this case.** This tricky code signal means you should apply all the cases and doctrines that you learned in class, as if they were the law of a fictional jurisdiction called 'State X'. However, you don't actually know anything about State X jurisprudence. Nobody does. Maybe their courts follow some minority positions, restatement views, or uniform laws. If there are multiple rules that could potentially be applied in a given situation, you might need to touch on all of them.

- **Potential twists:** Your professor may instead tell you that the law of a real jurisdiction (e.g., New York or Florida) applies. That obviously means that you should apply the actual law of those jurisdictions, and not waste time discussing cases and doctrines from other jurisdictions. However, if you see something tricky like "The law of *Floriduh* applies" this is probably a signal from the professor that you should use all cases and doctrines from the course regardless of their origin, but *favor* Florida rules if applicable.

Next, Read the Full Hypo without Taking Any Notes

Read the hypo once, to get a general sense of the characters and the story. Don't take notes just yet. There may be events that appear towards the end of the hypo that recolor issues you read at the beginning. If you start taking notes immediately, you may end up with a confusing mess because you don't have a good sense of the big picture.

Finally, Read the Hypo Again, Taking Detailed Notes as You Go

In the second reading, you will absorb the relevant details, and you can start taking good notes. Two readings is optimal for obtaining the most complete and accurate understanding of the hypo. This overlaps with step 2 below, on note taking.

"I Don't Have Time for This Much Reading"

I assume that you are saying this after doing many practice exams and evaluating your reading comprehension and speed, and not just because you are too scared to follow this advice. Good. Well, in that case you might just have to read the hypo once and start taking notes right away. It's not a big sacrifice, and it will probably allow you to pick up some extra time for the later steps.

Step 2: Issue Spotting/Note Taking

During your second reading of the hypo, you need to focus on issue spotting. Begin pulling out the operative facts and organizing them in a useful way. As you move into steps 3 and 4, you will be too focused on analysis and writing to waste time skimming the actual hypo text for your relevant facts. You'll get lost in that sea of words and waste valuable time. Instead, while the facts are fresh in your mind, make a cheat-sheet for future reference.

Taking Notes vs. Highlighting

Some students prefer to highlight the hypo text as they read, instead of taking notes. This can be effective, but I preferred taking notes on a separate piece of scrap paper.

Both techniques have advantages and disadvantages. Highlighting is definitely faster, but you may get confused when you reference back to the text. If the hypo is poorly written or confusing to begin with, covering the page with yellow marker won't do much to clarify it.

On the other hand, your own notes can be organized in any manner and can allow you to keep characters and events distinct in your mind. The downside is that it takes a little longer, and mistakes in your notes can cause big problems.

Ultimately, you need to make a personal decision about this step. You should find the right balance of speed, clarity, and accuracy. How do you figure out which technique is right for you? It starts with a "p" and ends with an "actice" and there's an "r" in the middle.

I'm going to show you the "actor-based" note technique that I used on my exams. It's different from the "timeline" approach that most students use (where events are outlined in the order that they occur in the hypo). The actor-based technique might work for you, or it might be completely confusing. Identifying what you like and dislike about this technique will help you create a method of your own.

The Actor-Based Note Style

Take a sheet of scrap paper. Every time a new character appears in the hypo write down his name. Leave some space below the name for details about his actions and status in the hypo. Keep a running list of all the characters and their actions, and make a special indication if they do something that would constitute a claim or defense in your essay.

Our Practice Hypo

We're going to work with this Torts hypo for the next few sections. You might want to put a bookmark here.

> Peter Palm attends Westo College and is a member of BKK frater-
> nity. BKK sponsored a flag-football[1] game against rival fraternity FGR,
> to benefit an orphanage. Peter also plays on the Westo college foot-
> ball team, as does FGR president Donny Dade.
>
> Recently, there has been tension between Peter and Donny. Ear-
> lier this week, Peter invited Donny's ex-girlfriend Brenda Broward
> over to the BKK fraternity house. Together, they posted a video on the
> internet in which Peter does a crude impersonation of Donny and
> then kisses Brenda for several minutes. Many Westo students have
> seen the video and have ridiculed Donny because of it.
>
> During the game, while Peter was running with the ball, Donny
> grabbed Peter by the shirt, and threw him to the ground. Donny said,
> "Sorry, I was trying to get the flag." Peter's shirt was ripped, but he
> was not hurt. Peter decided not to react because of the orphans in
> the stadium.
>
> On the next play, Peter caught the ball and Donny immediately
> tackled him hard around the waist. Peter lay on the ground gasping
> for air. Donny kicked him in the face, breaking his nose. "You're much
> more handsome on TV," said David.
>
> As Peter was carried off the field, the orphans cried hysterically.
>
> You are a junior associate at Bing, Ding, & Ring LLP. Peter has
> come to your office to ask about a possible lawsuit. Assume the laws
> of State X apply to this case. Please prepare a memo discussing the
> merits of his potential claims.

Technique in Action: Actor-based Note Sheet

If this were a real exam, you'd be taking notes on a sheet of
scrap paper as you read the hypo. It would look something like
this:

---

1. If you didn't grow up in America (or if you had a particularly
nerdy childhood), flag football is a less-violent variation of American
Football. Instead of tackling the ball carrier to end game play, you chase
the ball carrier, and snatch a small cloth flag hanging from his or her
waist. It is not considered to be a violent or "contact" sport.

Peter Palm
- Attends Wesco College
- BKK fraternity
- Plays college football
☆ IIED: Made crude video on web with Brenda ☆
- Not injured when thrown to the ground by Donny
- Nose broken by Donny's kick

Donny Dade
- FGR fraternity president
- Plays college football
- Brenda is ex-girlfriend
- Is ridiculed b/c of video
☆ BATTERY: Threw Peter to ground during football play
☆ BATTERY: Tackled Peter hard during FLAG football play
☆ BATTERY: Kicked Peter in face while on ground ☆
- Made insulting remark: "More handsome on TV..."

Brenda Broward
- Ex-girlfriend of Donny
☆ IIED: Made crude video on web w/ Peter ☆

Notice a Few Key Points about These Notes

The events and actions associated with each character are clearly separated. If you want to know who did what, you can find the information very quickly. Some of the events appear under more than one name. For example, the "crude video" action appears under both Brenda and Peter. When you are referencing back to these notes later, you might forget to look under Peter's heading for one of Brenda's actions. You'll avoid later confusion by just jotting down the event twice.

Most importantly, the actions that could form the basis of a tort claim are underlined and indicated with stars. You're definitely going to want to address each one of these issues in your essay. Remember, in this step of the writing process, you are *issue-spotting*; pulling out the legally operative facts and circumstances, and leaving behind any extraneous information. You will analyze these issues in the next step.

What's IIED?

The last item in the notes refers to a claim for "IIED," which stands for Intentional Infliction of Emotional Distress. It's a type of tort that involves intentionally inflicting emotional distress on a person (go figure). Your professor may not have covered it, because it is a relatively unimportant type of tort.

What about Those Poor Orphans?

The notes exclude the orphans completely, even though they appear several times in the hypo. That is because you are Peter's attorney, not some general legal analyst. If you had been hired by the orphans, you might have a claim against Donny for some form of emotional tort (although it would fail in most jurisdictions). Alternatively, if this was a contracts class, there might be a breach of contract claim by the orphans against the fraternities for failing to complete the game. That could involve Peter, but it's not relevant on a Torts exam.

The orphans don't factor into your essay at all, because they have no claim against Peter, and he has no claim against them. They are distracters, "red herrings," and you can ignore them completely.

Brenda did make it onto the notes page because she is more likely to be a player in some of the legal arguments. In fact, it turns out that she's not very important after all (she doesn't make it into the actual essay). If you're ever in doubt about the relevance of a character or fact, just include it. It's better to have too many notes than too few.

If You Have Time, Skim the Hypo Again Before Moving On

If you're a fast reader, you should give the hypo one more read through. It's very easy to miss an important fact or misread a significant word, and this final pass will catch those mistakes. If you're not fast enough for this final check, just move forward and have confidence that your notes are accurate enough to write a great essay. Nobody catches all the facts and professors know you are under pressure. Even the most critical grader will forgive minor or moderate mistakes based upon simple misreading.

Dealing with Spelling and Writing Errors in the Hypo

You may have noticed something strange at the end of the hypo.

> Peter lay on the ground gasping and Donny kicked him in the face, breaking his nose. "You're much more handsome on TV," said <u>David</u>.

Who the heck is David? Where did he come from? Is he just some annoying jerk who follows Peter around, making sarcastic comments at his expense? Is he Donny's evil twin brother, participating in an elaborate scheme to defraud the orphans?

David is obviously a typo. The professor meant to say Donny. Unfortunately, this happens all the time on law school exams. Many professors write their hypos quickly and carelessly, and don't proofread for mistakes. Often, they paste together segments of old exams, and leave behind confusing artifacts like accidental characters and inconsistent events.

What to Do When You Encounter an Error in the Hypo

Sometimes, it is really hard to know what the professor actually intended. Other times, the mistake is obvious and you can just work through it.

- **If the professor's intention is obvious:** Just write as if there was no mistake. In the Donny/David example above, you can completely ignore the mistake and attribute the comment to Donny. You might want to alert the professor that you saw the typo to show that you were paying close attention.

- **If the professor's intention is NOT obvious:** Make an assumption about the professor's probable intention and keep writing. Explain the error, explain why it's a problem, and then resolve the issue based on your assumption. Don't freeze or waste time trying to make sense of an unintentional error. Even worse, don't assume that the mistake will compel your professor to invalidate the entire question and give everyone a pass. You've got to write something.

An Example of a Major Error in the Hypo

Let's say the hypo has a mistake in the timeline: A character is in two places at once, which makes it impossible to resolve an important issue. First, make sure that there really is a mistake, and that you're not just misreading the hypo. If you're about 80% sure that there is a mistake, you need to explain what and where it is, and write your answer based on your best assumption of the professor's intention. For example, you might write something like this to resolve a timeline error:

> "There is a conflict in the timeline of the facts. In paragraph 1 line 10, Jones is at the gas station at 8:00 p.m. on Saturday. However, in paragraph 4, line 5 *at the same exact time*, he is at a birthday party forty miles away. Unless Jones has a time machine, the description of facts is probably inaccurate. For the purposes of my analysis, I will assume that he was at the birthday party first and then went to the gas station later. This appears to be the most logical assumption, given the sequence of other events."

Show the professor her mistake, with exact citations to the hypo. She may not be aware that there is an error. Even if you are wrong about the mistake (in other words, the hypo is correct, you just misread it), the professor might see how her own wording was confusing and give you partial credit.

Next, make an assumption about the professor's probable intention. Birthday party first, gas station second. You might be wrong — your professor intended events to progress in the opposite order. But she can't blame you for making a wrong assumption, because she made the mistake. You will probably get full credit for your analysis, even though you made the wrong guess. Most professors will be impressed that you weren't flustered by their mistake and were able to continue your analysis anyway. That's what real lawyers do.

Step 3: Organized Analysis/ Outlining a Roadmap

You're not done with your scrap paper just yet. Before you start writing the actual essay, you should organize your arguments into some kind of outline or "roadmap." Putting this much effort into your scrap paper may seem like a waste of time, but it's not. Remember, we're trying to do one thing at a time. Good lawyers don't just walk into court and start arguing off the top of their heads; they plan each argument carefully before they open their mouths.

When you finally begin to write the essay, the roadmap will keep you on course. If you lose your train of thought while searching for a word or contemplating a semi-colon — just turn back to your roadmap and get back on track. It is critical to have a plan before you start writing.

The Roadmap _IS_ Your Essay

The roadmap is your entire essay, written in shorthand code. Every argument is prepared at this stage, but you don't waste time with grammar, spelling, or legibility. When you get to the actual writing stage, your only task will be to translate this personal code into a language that your professor can understand.

How to Structure Your Roadmap

You might organize your roadmap by party, by claim, or chronologically. It doesn't really matter how you organize the roadmap, as long as your method is consistent. Pick a structure that makes logical sense in the context of the hypo, because your essay will ultimately follow the roadmap.

Sample Organization Plan:

Peter's Claims:
- Battery vs. Donny (thrown to ground/shirt ripped)
- Battery vs. Donny (hard tackle)
- Battery vs. Donny (kick to face)

Donny's Claims:
- Intentional Infliction of Emotional Distress (IIED) vs. Peter/Brenda (internet video)

Make Your Roadmap in IRAHNC Format

If you're going to write in IRAHNC format, you should outline that way too. It will help you stay focused during the writing stage. Go through each claim and repeat the IRAHNC steps. Include just enough information so that *you* understand the outline. Don't waste time writing out all the facts or elements of each claim. Just point out the relevant facts and then sketch your arguments, counter-arguments, and rebuttals.

Practice Makes Fast

You might spend 50–60% of the allotted time for each essay just working on your scrap paper. That's okay. The more you practice, the faster it gets.

Sample Segment of a Roadmap Outline:

Claims: P v D

1) Battery: throw/rip shirt
I: claim of battery
R: harmful/offensive contact
A: D grabbed shirt, threw P to the ground. Prob. qualifies as harm. offens. contact. Only touched clothes, but prob. sufficient (cite to HIGGS case).
H: Consent to harm. offens. contact by playing sport. Both P and D are athletes so they knew risk. Grabbing shirt while trying to get flag could be accident - avg. player might expect.
N: Might be beyond <u>scope</u> of consent b/c flag football doesn't involve much rough contact. Plus, later events suggest it wasn't an accident.
C: P prob. prevails on this claim, but it could have been an accident.

2) Battery: hard tackle
I: claim of battery
R: same as #1
A: D tackled P hard around the waist. Seems pretty harmful...
H: Same as #1. Consent to harm. offens. contact by playing sport.
N: This is more likely to be beyond the scope of consent b/c tackling not expected in FLAG football. Too rough and later events suggest intent to harm.
C: P fairly likely to prevail on this claim.

Step 4: Presentation/Writing

By the time you actually start writing the essay, the most difficult parts of the process are already finished. You understand the fact pattern, you've identified all of the issues, and you've basically written the entire essay on scrap paper. Now you just follow the roadmap. Stick to the IRAHNC format and flesh out your shorthand into a complete essay. If an issue or argument suddenly occurs to you while writing, just add it in, and then return to the roadmap.

It Ain't Gotta Be Pretty

Clarity and organization are the most important aspects of a successful law school essay. Don't worry about grammar or spelling (unless you have *one of those* professors ... and you will know if you do). You shouldn't waste time revising the style of your essay or correcting awkward word choices. If a sentence communicates your intention with reasonable clarity, it's good enough.

If you accidentally write something *really* confusing, just explain what you meant instead of correcting what you wrote. For example:

> In order for Peter to prevail in a battery claim, he will need to demonstrate that the touch he experienced as a result of Donny's action was either harmful to him or else offensive. *In other words*, Donny's tackle must have constituted a harmful or offensive contact.

That first sentence barely makes sense, even though it is technically correct. Rather than trying to untie that knot by re-writing the sentence, just re-state your meaning in a clearer way. That will save you time and frustration as you race against the clock on exam day.

Let's see how our roadmap would translate into a completed essay segment:

Claims: Peter (P) v. Donny (D)

1) Battery: Throw/Ripped Shirt

P may wish to bring a claim against D for battery. At common law, the tort of battery is defined as the harmful or offensive touching of another person. Here, D grabbed P's shirt during a football game and threw P to the ground. Although D only touched P's clothes and not his actual body, this is probably sufficient to qualify as a battery. In

---

HIGGS,[2] the court evaluated a similar situation. There, the defendant swung his fist at the plaintiff and knocked off the plaintiff's hat. The court there held that harmful or offensive contact with another person's *clothing* was sufficient to constitute harmful or offensive contact to that person. Here, D's act of grabbing P's shirt is probably sufficiently similar to the defendant's action in HIGGS. As a result, D's act is probably sufficient to constitute a battery, even though D only touched P's clothes.

However, D may counter-argue that P consented to some degree of harmful or offensive contact by choosing to play in a flag football game. Consent is an affirmative defense to the tort of battery. D may argue that since P was an athlete (on the college football team), P was aware of the risk of accidental harmful contact when playing sports, yet P agreed to play anyway. Moreover, the average player in a flag football game might expect to have his outer clothing grabbed during an attempt to seize the flag.

Nevertheless, D's action might be beyond the *scope* of P's consent. P probably expected that he might accidentally be grabbed by the shirt during play, but probably did not expect to be thrown by his shirt with enough force to rip it. Moreover, subsequent events suggest that D acted intentionally, not accidentally. An intentional act of violence is probably outside the scope of P's consent in a friendly sporting event. P will probably prevail in this claim, unless the judge determines that D's action was an accident.

2) Battery: Hard Tackle

P may also wish to bring a second battery claim against D. The tort of battery is defined in section 1 above. Later in the game, D tackled P hard around the waist and knocked him to the ground. In most circumstances, this kind of contact would almost certainly be considered harmful touching. However, D may attempt to use the same counter argument as above — P consented to some level of physical contact by agreeing to play in a flag football game. Nevertheless, D is very unlikely to succeed in this defense, because a hard tackle is almost certainly outside the scope of consent in a flag football game. The very purpose of playing *flag* football is to avoid tack-

---

2. A fictional case that I made up for this hypo. Please don't cite to "Higgs" on your actual torts exam.

ling and rough contact. The fact that D kicked P after tackling him suggests that this tackle was intended to harm P, and was not accidental, or part of the game. Therefore, P is very likely to succeed in this battery claim.

Section IV

The Finishing Touches

Writing an exam is more than just blindly applying IRAHNC over and over. I wish it were that simple, but there are a lot of elements in play and very few absolute rules. Here are some tricks and tips to put the final polish on your exam writing strategy.

A. Abbreviate Everything

Most professors (but not all) will allow you to abbreviate words in your essay. For example, you can call your plaintiff "P" and your defendant "D." Most professors will even accept abbreviations like "neg." for negligence, or "juris." for jurisdiction. Every second counts, so abbreviate if you can. Just make sure your abbreviations are clear by explaining their meaning somewhere in the essay.

Don't get carried away though. If your essay starts to look like a text message from a fourteen-year-old girl, your aged professor may not be able to follow it. "D will prbly R-gue dat but-4 cAuZa-TiOn is lacking b/c he's lame :-) OMG ROFL."

B. Stick to a Formula

If your essay is rambling and disorganized, the professor will quickly lose her patience and put it straight in the C+ pile. On the other hand, if your essay has a formulaic and predictable style, she's much more likely to follow your arguments and grade favorably.

For example, think about a time when you heard a really catchy new song on the radio. Even though you've never heard it before, it starts to stick in your head immediately. By the time the chorus rolls around for the third time, you can sing along, because you've already picked up the rhythm. On law school exams, you want your professor to sing along with you. By the third time she sees your IRAHNC formula, she's going to say to herself, "Okay, there's a formula. I see where this is going." Your essay has a rhythm, which makes it easy to read, and easy to grade.

If you're not going to use IRAHNC, you should find some other formula that suits you, and repeat it over and over in your essay. This is not a creative writing course—you will not be penalized for having a repetitive style. It's much more important to be clear than interesting.

C. Use Headings, Bullet Points, Numbers, Underlines, etc.

If you make your professor's life easier, she will reward you. A ten-page, single-spaced, solid block of words is going to make her eyes roll back into her head. Break up the page with headings, titles, bullet points, and lists. Yes, I'm telling you to put them in your actual essay. Categorize everything into cohesive, single topic segments. Put a big heading at the top of each segment that screams: "Hey look over here! Now I'm going to talk about this issue." For an example, see my sample essay segment above on page 53.

D. The Power of Probably

In the world of exam writing, there is only one acceptable absolute statement: *Never* make an absolute statement! Every argument should be softened with words like "probably," "maybe," or "most likely." No matter how thoroughly you analyze an issue, it is impossible to predict the outcome of litigation. Your essay should be filled with phrases like: "Peter *may* assert …"; "Donny *probably* won't succeed in this argument ..."; "A judge will *almost certainly* reject ..."; etc.

E. Big Trap: Outline Dumping

If there is one thing that professors universally despise, it is the "outline dump." This is where a student crams everything that she knows into her essay, regardless of the facts presented in the hypo. The issue-spotter exam is not a forum to demonstrate how much material you have memorized. You must limit your analysis to the issues that are actually presented in the hypo. There are two types of students who perform the outline dump:

The Over-Prepared Dumper

In some classes, you'll spend several weeks covering a particular topic that seems important and fundamental to the course. But surprisingly, when you take the exam, you don't see any questions or hypos addressing that topic.

The Over-Prepared Dumper gets anxious when this happens. She studied really hard, and she wants to show the professor that she understands every topic in the course. As a result, she stretches the facts, looking for long-shot arguments and excuses to work them in.

That's a mistake. It is very likely that at least 20–40% of the course material won't be on your exam. Professors focus their exam questions on topics that are difficult to analyze, easy to test, or just plain interesting. Several topics will be intentionally excluded.

The Under-Prepared Dumper

The Under-Prepared Dumper didn't study hard enough. On the exam, she's confronted with a topic that she knows absolutely nothing about. Rather than leave the page blank, she writes about some other topic instead. Unfortunately, that topic is completely irrelevant to the facts presented.

Don't fall into this trap either. You've got to know every topic that was assigned in the course. You can't fake your way through an issue-spotter exam. Your professor will see through your attempt to divert his attention and penalize you for it.

F. Time Is a Factor

You must budget your time well. Here are some tips to reduce wasted time:

Practice, Practice, Practice, Practice

The more you practice writing exams, the less time will be a factor on exam day. Familiarity with the testing format will make you comfortable and keep you focused. You will know how to allocate your time, and you will develop an instinct for budgeting those precious minutes towards the end. Most importantly, you will re-use many of the analytical structures and tricks that you developed during practice. You'll spend less time thinking and more time writing, because much of the hard work is already done.

Follow the Professor's Suggested Time Allotments

Often, professors will give you a continuous block of time for taking the entire exam (usually about four hours), but they will suggest time periods for individual questions or test-segments. For example, a professor might suggest that you spend one hour on the first essay, thirty minutes on the next two, and one hour on a multiple choice section.

These time suggestions tend to be gross underestimations. The professor may suggest thirty minutes for a question that should probably take ninety minutes to complete. But I strongly suggest that you follow their time suggestions anyway. Why? Because when a professor says to spend thirty minutes on a question, they are really saying *"There are only thirty minutes worth of* points *in this question."* The professor has not only sliced up the exam into suggested times, she's probably also sliced it up into relative point values. So you are well advised to follow her instructions, if possible.

Don't Be Afraid to Bail Out

If you're forty-five minutes into a question that had a suggested time of thirty minutes, you need to just stop. Wrap it up, wherever it is, and move on to the next question. If you skipped some of the minor issues entirely, don't worry about it. If you missed some important issues, work them in as best you can in two or three sentences and then bail.

When you push over into the time allocated for other questions, you start shaving serious points from your overall grade. Wrap it up as quickly as possible and start fresh on the next question. Most likely, you'll pick up more points by attacking the next question than you would by putting any more energy into the current one. Remember, no points will be awarded for an unanswered question, but you'll probably get good partial credit for a well-reasoned but unfinished essay.

When You Finish a Question

Move on. You probably won't have time to proofread each answer as you go. If you finish the entire exam ahead of schedule, you may want to go through your answers and clean up some of your arguments. Trust your notes, trust your roadmap, and trust your instincts. There are usually more points ahead of you than there are behind you.

G. Open Book Exams

Having your casebook, outlines, and supplements is like carrying a parachute and a life jacket on an airplane—hopefully you won't need them, but you've got them just in case. Having an open book exam can be a big trap. Professors often make open book exams more difficult and may have higher expectations about the quality of your answers. So don't get too excited.

You absolutely won't have time to do serious research or referencing during the test, no matter how well you tab and highlight your materials. You should study just as hard as you would for a closed book test. If you plan to use your outlines or supplements as references during the test, I strongly suggest that you practice using those materials a few times before the big day. Take a practice exam and see how long it takes to look things up. Get a preview of which materials will be useful and which will frustrate you when the clock is running.

H. Waving the Flag

One of the best tricks in exam writing is called "flagging"—bringing attention to an issue without performing a full analysis. Sometimes, a fact in the hypo will partially indicate a legal issue, but your professor didn't provide enough information to resolve it fully. For example, you may spot two elements of a tort, but the third critical element is missing. You can't just assume that the third element is present, but you don't want to ignore the issue entirely. All you have to do is flag it. For example:

> "It is also possible that Franklin has a claim for Intentional Infliction of Emotional Distress (IIED) because the sales clerk loudly berated him with racial slurs in front of his children. However, we don't know if Franklin experienced severe emotional distress as a result of the incident, which is required for a claim of IIED. More research is needed into this issue."

Franklin would like to bring this claim, but we don't know if he can. Since the facts didn't tell us how he felt after the incident (a critical element of IIED), we need to ask him. Since this is an exam (and Franklin is a fictional character) we can't do that. You can't invent new facts, and you shouldn't do a full analysis. Just flag the issue, and move on. You'll probably pick up a few bonus points.

Gaps in the Law

Occasionally, you will confront issues that fall into "legal gaps." This occurs when courts across the country have failed to reach a consensus on a particular legal concept or rule. You may have heard of instances when there is a "majority" and "minority" split amongst the states—most states say the rule should be X, but some others say the rule should be Y. Both rules are valid, but you don't always know which one to apply on an exam.

If your professor doesn't tell you which rule to follow, you must indicate on your exam that you've fallen into a legal gap. This is not a problem, especially if you were smart enough to study both rules ahead of time.

One easy way to deal with a legal gap is to use the minority view as a counter-argument. For example, you can set up your initial arguments using only the majority view and when it comes time for your counter-arguments, you can say something like this:

> "However, if this jurisdiction follows the minority view with respect to consent, it may be necessary to show that Jones verbally expressed his willingness to participate. Since Jones remained silent when the procedure began, he may not have offered sufficient consent. More research is needed to determine whether this jurisdiction follows the majority or minority approach."

We don't know which rule to follow in this imaginary jurisdiction. If the minority rule is applied, it will seriously affect the outcome of our case. It's too important to ignore, but we also don't want to get dragged into writing our entire essay over again from the alternative perspective. Just point out that a split in legal doctrine exists, and if the minority view is applied, it will affect the outcome. Tell the professor that you don't know which rule to follow, and that it is very important to research the issue more.

I. Red Herrings

A "red herring" is a fact that appears to be legally significant, but in reality, is just meaningless. Sometimes red herrings appear unintentionally because the professor failed to realize that a fact is misleading. Occasionally, professors include them intentionally to distract, trick, or trap you. Red herrings are relatively rare on exams, so you should generally assume that *all* facts are legally operative and significant to your analysis.

When fishing for red herrings, look for:

- Issues that don't involve the party that you represent
- Issues that are outside the scope of the exam instructions
- Issues that are outside the scope of the course
- Issues that are totally absurd

If you see an obvious red herring, just ignore it. If you are unsure, explain why in your essay. Tell the professor what additional information you'd need in order to clarify the situation. Just don't say, "I know that fact about the washing machine was a red herring. Nice try professor, but I'm too clever for your petty tricks." Even if it was a red herring, you'll get no points for that.

J. The Impossible Question

Let's say you start reading question #4 in the exam booklet and your palms suddenly start to sweat. You have no idea where to begin with this bad boy. Did they hand you the wrong exam booklet? Are you in the wrong room? The question is impossible.

When you are totally stumped, just write. Write anything. Don't outline, don't think too much, and don't get paralyzed with anxiety. Write about cases you remember, write about things your professor said in class. If you are really stuck, try bending (or mutilating) an unrelated legal doctrine to fit the situation. At least show that you have identified an issue and attempted to address it.

You'll be surprised at how much credit you will earn for this. Sometimes, the professor is deliberately asking you a question that cannot be answered. They toss you something crazy, experimental, or just plain, hard and they want to see how you respond. If this occurs, you will get credit for creativity. At the very least, rest assured that most other students in the class are stumped too, and the question probably won't factor heavily in the curve.

Section V

Working Throughout the Semester

Every homework assignment, every reading, every class lecture, and every study-group session is part of your exam preparation. You're going to need the entire semester to get ready, so you should start studying on the first day of class. Stretching the exam preparation process over the entire semester will make you more focused on a daily basis, and more relaxed as the exam gets closer. But that is easier said than done. Law school is hard and it takes tremendous patience and perseverance to stay on target.

Boiling Point

When I was a 1L, I vaguely pictured the Law Review office as a place where smartly dressed young men and women debated the significance of that afternoon's Supreme Court decision. So imagine my disillusionment when I discovered that it is actually just a place to eat stale pizza and check your email. That was fine with me. I was too busy reading old Supreme Court cases for my Conlaw class to really bother with the new ones.

I tried to keep a pretty laid-back attitude during law school. I worked hard because I enjoyed the process, but I never let my stress level get too high. After two or three semesters, I had established a routine and I had confidence in my method. My classes were no longer a stress factor. It was everything else in my life that drove me crazy.

In exchange for the gold star on your resume, the Law Review asks a lot in return. We didn't debate the dynamics of jurisprudence, but we did spend many hours arguing over the proper use of *infra* in legal citations. We checked hundreds of facts, thousands of citations, and millions of punctuation marks. I was finally standing on steady ground in my classes, but suddenly I had Law Review editors breathing down my neck, not to mention clubs, job interviews, friends, networking events, and face-time with faculty. I couldn't just hide in some corner of the library with my books anymore—I had to be an actual human being out in the sunlight.

I dropped everything when I came to law school—job, home, friends, family. Now my life was starting to grow back, whether I liked it or not, and it was messing up my newfound rhythm.

One day I was in the law review office, eating stale pizza and checking my email. An *Articles and Comments* editor named Alvin came panting into the office with a huge stack of books and papers.

"Are you ok, man?" I asked. "You look kind of worn out."

"Yeah, I'm fine. Well, no not really. Thanks for asking," he said.

"Do you need help with something?"

"No, I've just got a lot of work to do for the Review and my client at the clinic is probably going to jail. Plus, I'm taking insane classes this semester," he said. He shelved the books into a confusing system of bins and baskets for later reference.

"Maybe you should take a break? Do some of this stuff tomorrow," I suggested.

"You're never going to have less work than you have today. Responsibilities only go in one direction—up," he said. "I may as well do it all now, because it will only be worse tomorrow. See ya."

"Jeez. That guy needs some time off," I awkwardly joked to the room. But inside I was sad to admit that I agreed with him. Sometimes it was really hard to keep things below boil.

A. Set Your Sights on the Exam

You're going to have millions of things competing for your attention, but you can't lose focus. Besides your social life and extracurricular activities, even things like attending class and study groups can be a big time drain. It's so easy to get bogged down in a daily routine. Your school work gets parsed into weeks, days, and hours, causing you to lose your sense of the big picture.

B. My Philosophy—
"More Work, Less Thinking"

When you encounter a difficult topic or a complicated case, you can spend hours trying to unravel it. Maybe you will figure it out, and maybe you won't, but you've wasted a lot of time in the endeavor. There are more effective ways to spend your study time.

Very often, the source of confusion is not the subject matter, but the presentation—either in your books or in class lectures. If your study resources leave you confused and frustrated, you need to find other materials that provide a clearer presentation. You need **supplements**.

As you move through the semester, you'll be combing through huge amounts of information from books and lectures. Some of it is important, but a lot of it is junk. The litmus test is whether the information will be useful on your exam, but unfortunately, you can't always assess that early in the semester. You will gain the proper instincts for this as you develop the skill of effective **note taking**.

Additionally, you will encounter some topics that are just plain hard (for example, the *rule against perpetuities*, or the *Erie doctrine*), and even the best supplementary texts won't be able to explain them clearly. In other situations, you might understand a handful of individual topics, but fail to see the cross-references and conceptual overview. You need to take a step back from your reading and put the material into your own words. This is the role of **outlining**.

Using supplements, taking really good notes, and making your own outlines will require more *physical effort* than just reading the assigned cases and hiding under your desk in class. You'll have to read more, write more, and spend a lot of time organizing your material. But the process will require less *mental effort* than the scattered method adopted by most law students. It's methodical, controlled, and pre-planned.

Law school will become like a big jigsaw puzzle—find the right pieces and then take the time to assemble them. It can be tedious, and very challenging, but with enough time and perseverance you will eventually see the picture.

C. Your Toolbox of Law School Supplements

Every class is different, but most will require you to read beyond the syllabus in order to master the material. In some particularly challenging classes (for example, Civil Procedure, Secured Transactions, or Federal Income Tax) supplements are practically a requirement. There are a few progressive professors who recognize the value of supplementary texts and will recommend a few good ones in the syllabus. But the vast majority of professors regard supplementary texts with disdain, perhaps because they depart stylistically from the traditional flavor of common law legal education.

You should use your own judgment about whether to rely on supplements and which ones to choose. In some courses, you may feel that your casebook is actually doing a good job and supplements will only muddy the waters. But it is important to remember that your professor chose the assigned texts because *in her opinion* they are effective teaching tools. You are free to disagree about the quality of the assigned texts, and you shouldn't only rely on your professor's selection of books.

Supplements come in a variety of shapes and sizes, and different books play different roles in your study routine. Some are everyday workhorses, and others are good for occasional reference. Finding the right mix is a matter of personal preference and budget.

Despite the well-established benefits of supplements, some students continue to resist them. Here are the excuses that I hear most frequently:

- "I can barely finish my assigned reading! I don't have time to read another book." *False.* Supplements will probably make your reading time go faster, and you may even be able to reduce the time you spend with your casebook.
- "Supplements are cheating." *False.* Check your school's honor code. If your school has not banned the use of supplements, it is not cheating to use them. If you are unsure, ask the dean of students or academic support director. Most successful law students use some form of supplementary text to assist in their exam preparation.
- "There is no supplement available for my casebook." *False.* While some types of supplements are tailored to specific casebooks, most are not. Instead, they are "generic commercial outlines," covering entire subject areas from start to finish. They can be used regardless of what textbook or casebook your professor assigned.
- "If I use supplements, I won't learn the material in the way my professor intends. It will just confuse me." *False.* Professors like to think that their curriculum is unique and that their teaching style is revolutionary. In reality, every Torts class at every law school in the country is almost exactly the same. You will cover the same four or five topics, the same rules, and many of the same cases. The minor divergences among syllabi are insignificant. Your supplement doesn't replace your casebook or your professor's lecture. It *supplements* your primary materials, and will help you understand the most confusing issues and concepts with ease.
- "My professor said that supplements are useless for his class." *Probably false.* Some professors have a revulsion to supplements that borders on hysteria.[1] For whatever reason,

---

1. In one class, I was adamantly warned that using supplementary texts would cause me to misunderstand all of the course material and lead to a failing grade (presumably followed by a life of professional and personal failure). In particular, we were warned not to even look at a very popular treatise on the topic. So naturally, I read the forbidden

your professor may have warned you against using supplements in her class. This might actually be true; some classes are not conducive to supplements, or there are simply no good supplements available. *But don't take your professor's word for it.* Ask students who have previously taken the class, and check out the available supplements for yourself. Take charge of your learning.

- **"I can't afford to buy all of these books."** *Maybe.* This is the only excuse that is somewhat reasonable, but in my opinion supplements are worth the extra money. Many online stores sell used textbooks and supplements at drastically reduced prices, so do some research before you decide against buying more books.

D. Taking Notes (from Readings and in Class)

The Illusion of Hard Work

Whenever I did a reading assignment, I set out my laptop, my casebook, two supplements, and my bookstand. I was furiously pounding notes into the keyboard, pausing only to sip my latte or adjust my glasses. If you saw me in the library, you would probably think, "Here is a specimen of *Nerdius Nofriendhavium.* This species is nearly extinct because the males seldom find an opportunity to reproduce."

But as much as it looked like I was hard at work, I was actually being extremely lazy. I wasn't wrestling with the great ideas of twentieth-century jurisprudence or writing a revolutionary manifesto on legal reform; I was just copying down whatever the

---

treatise, as well as several other books on her evil list, and found them immensely helpful. On the other hand, I found the casebook she selected to be muddled, misguided, and extremely boring, and I threw it in the back of my closet. Needless to say, I got an *A* on her exam, and my life has yet to spiral into personal catastrophe.

books said, even if I had no idea what it meant. The better my notes were, the less I had to struggle.

The Illusion of Paying Attention in Class

I didn't have to pay attention in class because professors rarely said anything that wasn't already in my notes. Everything in their lecture could be found somewhere in the casebook or one of my supplements (which I had faithfully summarized the night before in my notes). I just scrolled along with their lectures like a teleprompter, listening with one ear in case they happened to drop a clue about the exam. If I got called on, I would ask the professor to repeat the question and then just read the next line out of my notes. This always worked, so I looked like a teacher's pet in addition to a loser.

More Work, Less Effort

Doing reading assignments took me a long time. But there was very little *effort* involved. I just read my book and wrote down whatever the author said, condensing the details by about 60%. If I didn't understand something, I just copied it down anyway, and made a note to ask the professor. Why should I waste time figuring it out myself when this lady stands up in class every day and answers questions from the audience? More importantly, she'll explain how *she* understands and interprets the concept, which is the only way that matters for *her* exam.

Your Notes Are Part of Exam Preparation

Let's say you read a really hard case for your Property class. After reading it three times, and discussing it with your roommate, you think you've got a pretty good grip on it and you're ready for class tomorrow. Wonderful. Will you remember any of this information three months from now when you sit down to take the exam? Better yet, will you remember it three days from now after reading a dozen more cases for your other classes? If you don't have a photographic memory, you need good notes to prepare for an exam. There's too much information and you won't be able to keep the details straight. Set it all down in writing while it's fresh in your mind.

Note Taking Is a Personal Matter

Some students insist on writing everything by hand, while others use laptops. Many students take all of their notes from the class lectures, while other students take notes from the book and just listen in class. There's no absolute rule on note taking, and this is one area where my method may not be any better than yours. However, when deciding how to handle this important element of exam preparation, keep two things in mind:

> 1) **"What weaknesses as a student can I overcome by taking notes in a particular way?"** Your note taking should compensate for your weaknesses as a student, such as lack of organization, time management, or reading comprehension. Personally, my biggest weakness was long-term memory, and I structured my notes to compensate for this.
>
> 2) **"How will this method of note-taking help me on my exam?"** Look critically at your notes from the semester so far. Are they too skeletal to refresh your memory? Are they so dense that you can't tolerate re-reading them? If your notes won't help you prepare for the exam, your notes are not accomplishing their task.

E. Outlining

When you make an outline, you synthesize your notes into a cohesive "master document" that contains everything you know about the course. Outlining is not an absolute requirement for success, but it will really help. Students usually avoid it for the wrong reasons, mainly the amount of work involved.

"What Is an Outline?"

Think of it as your personalized study manual. Everything that you want to know for the exam should be included. Anything that is confusing should be broken down and clarified so that you can easily review it later. Anything that you think is superfluous should be ruthlessly cut out. Essentially, it is a summary of the course in your own words.

Making an outline is extremely student-specific. For some students, it should be dense and full of details. For others, it should be a minimal and sparse. What makes your outline so effective is its personal nature. Try thinking of it like this:

- **During the semester you *intake* material.** The substance of the course is fed to you by your professor and the casebook author. The problem is, everything is presented to suit *their* tastes, not yours. The pieces of the puzzle are all there, but the way it is assembled may not make sense. This is the note taking phase; you collect the puzzle pieces, with the intention of reorganizing them later.

- **Later, you *output* that same material in a format that better suits your taste.** You take all those puzzle pieces—the cases, black-letter rules, and policy arguments—and you re-organize them into a structure and language that makes sense to you. This is the outlining phase; you assemble the puzzle.

- **Then finally, you *re-intake* the material right before the exam.** As the exam approaches, you study from your personalized outline, rather than your raw notes and casebook. You're looking at the same information as everyone else, but it's assembled in a new format that is tailor-made for your personal sensibilities. You have internalized the subject and made it your own. **Your outline reflects how *you* would have taught the course if *you* were the professor.** It's a thousand times more effective than just re-reading notes or cases.

You need to decide exactly what goes into the outline and how it should be organized. If drawing cartoons instead of writing makes sense, don't be afraid to do that.

"So, I Just Print Out All My Class Notes, Right?"

No! What did I just say?! When most students talk about their "outline" they mean their raw, unedited notes from the book and class lectures. They call this scrambled, unorganized stack of paper an outline. If you really want to master the material, you need to *make something* out of this stack of paper, not just print it out. You need to assemble the puzzle.

"Ok, I Get It. But ... Why Can't I Just Use My Notes?"

Alright, I give up, you can. If your notes are good and the structure and organization makes sense, why waste time doing anything more? But there are additional benefits to synthesizing your notes into a streamlined new document that make it worth the time and trouble:

- The process of outlining is a great way to review the entire course from start to finish. You will really test the limits of your understanding by creating something with your notes, rather than just reading them.

- Outlining forces you to review the material multiple times and in different ways. It will greatly increase your confidence.

- In the final hours before your exam, you need resources that you can read and absorb quickly. Nothing beats an outline, written in your own words.

- If you have an open book exam, it is critical to have everything at your fingertips. You cannot afford to waste valuable time searching for a case or rule in your notes. Keeping this in mind, you can deliberately format your outline for extra-fast reference.

"My Cousin Is a 3L at [Prestigious Law School] and She Said Outlining Is a Waste of Time"

You're going to get a lot of advice on how to study for exams and some if it is going to be really helpful. But, if you take anything away from this section, remember that *effective studying is personal*. What I did, what your cousin did, what your professor did—that's useful advice to help you get on track, but it's not the solution. When it comes to studying, play to your *weaknesses*. Figure out where the gaps are in your abilities as a student, and then use your study time and techniques to compensate for that. If you don't know where to begin, follow my suggestions for a while. That will give you an objective basis for comparison. Eventually you will discover how to do things in your own way. Listen to your cousin, listen to me, but most of all, start listening to your own good instincts.

F. A Sample Semester

Everyone feels nervous as the exam approaches. But for those students who have used the semester wisely, there is a deep confidence running beneath the agitated surface.

Every lecture, every reading, every practice test—it's all training for the big event. If thinking that way makes you even more nervous, it shouldn't. Let's say you were assigned a big research project instead of an exam. Would you rather have one week to write it, or three months? This process is no different.

How can you maximize your study time? How can you keep the exam in focus throughout the semester? Here is a sample semester, with some suggestions about how to budget your time:

Weekdays

A lot of study time gets lost during the week just by attending class, socializing with friends, going to the gym, and taking necessary relaxation breaks. That's okay; you need all of these things to support your intensive study time. Just keep control of your schedule and don't let the diversions get out of hand. During the day, attend your classes and use your break time between lectures wisely. A one-hour break should be filled with resting, eating, and socializing. A three-hour break should be used for studying.

During the week, your main objective should be getting all of your assignments completed and staying on-pace with the class lectures.

Weekends

It is critical to work on the weekend if you plan to really increase your exam performance. You should use the weekends to get ahead in your reading assignments. This will relieve some pressure during the upcoming week. Most importantly, this is your chance to read your supplements, and to do practice exams.

The Middle of the Semester

By mid-semester, it's time to start thinking about outlines. It usually took me four to six weeks to complete all of my outlines. Some students like to make their outlines later in the semester and complete them all in a matter of days. Their theory is that intensive outlining right before the exam will keep the material fresh in their minds. While this may work for some people, in my opinion, completing an entire outline in four days is way too ambitious and creates artificial pressure. It sounds a lot like cramming to me, which we have already established is ineffective. A better approach is to start your outline several weeks in advance—when you still have plenty of time to do it right.

Mid-semester is also time to begin doing practice exams seriously. Get a friend to work with, or just lock yourself in your bedroom for a few hours. Don't be scared, and don't take it too seriously. Just start and see where it takes you.

Spring Break, Thanksgiving Recess, and Other Breaks

An extended break from class is really valuable. While you might feel like taking a much needed (and deserved) break to watch TV, relax with family, and catch up with friends, I advise you to budget this time very carefully. These rare breaks often come at critical times in the semester, perhaps only a few weeks before your test. Use the time for serious work, not just having fun. You might want to do practice exams or put a big dent in your outlines. Personally, I liked to use school recesses to get *way* ahead in my reading assignments.

During one spring break, my friend Kevin and I stayed in his tiny New York City apartment for an entire week without leaving. We studied for about 10 to 13 hours a day, subsisting on hummus dip, iced tea, and quesadillas. In six days I completed four weeks' worth of reading assignments (thanks to some very good supplementary texts). When I got back to school, I was so far ahead in class that it was torturously boring to sit through lectures. I was focused on more important things like taking practice exams and perfecting my outline. Was it a fun spring break? Not really. But it's over now and I'll never have to do it again.

The "Reading" Period

If your law school is generous enough to provide a designated "reading period" before each exam, you should plan to make maximum use of it. You might also have a few gap days between each exam, and that time must be used for serious studying. If you don't have an official reading period before your first exam, just make one for yourself: Double your efforts and complete the syllabus a few days ahead of schedule. Make a study schedule, and stick to it. You don't want to waste this time.

Example: A Three-Day Reading Period

If you have a three-day break between each exam, here is a suggested schedule for allocating your time and effort.

- **Day One:** Your goal on day one is to get a birds-eye view of the entire course. Focus your review on the big picture — the major topics and general structure of the course. Hopefully your outline is already complete, and you can spend this day just reading and refreshing your memory. If you haven't completed your outline, use this day to do so (try to leave enough time for at least one skim in the evening). If you're not planning to make an outline, read your notes from books and class.

- **Day Two:** Split the daytime hours between re-reading your outline (or notes) and carefully working with a good commercial supplement. If anything in your outline or supplement confuses you, take the time to clarify it with new notes in the margin. In the evening, do two practice exam essays. Don't stress about the time or closed book requirements when practicing. Write solid answers with your notes open to boost your confidence and work out some of the difficult concepts and recurring issues.

- **Day Three:** You should devote the final day before an exam to serious practice. Do at least two full exams in real test conditions (e.g., closed book with the actual time limit). Spend the rest of the afternoon doing additional practice hypos—even if you just sketch out your answers on scrap paper. Do as many practice exams as possible during this time. Spend the early evening reviewing your outline, focusing on the most difficult topics. If you'll be using a laptop to take the exam, make sure that any required software is installed and working properly. Don't forget to pack your laptop power cable for the next day (I forgot it once and it was terrifying). Have a good dinner and go to bed at a reasonable time. Set two alarms.

- **After the exam:** Now that the test is over, you've got to spend some time relaxing. Taking a law school exam is a big accomplishment, regardless of your grade. For better or worse, your fate is sealed, so just forget about it. If you can afford a break, try to take the rest of the day off. See a movie, hang out with friends who aren't in law school, or just pass out on the couch. Exams are a marathon; if you use up all your steam on the first test, you'll never make it to the fifth.

"When Should I Re-read My Casebook?"

Never. When you're three days away from the exam, you might as well throw the casebook in the trash. You will need resources

that are easy to read, condensed, and well-organized (three quali-
ties that most casebooks lack).

If you have your own outline, that should be your primary re-
source during finals. If you didn't make an outline, use a commercial outline. If you need to review individual cases, use your
own briefs or "canned briefs" (pre-made briefs that are sold as
companions to various popular casebooks. Ask for help at your
law bookstore.). Reading a full-text Supreme Court opinion
could take three hours. Reading a brief takes about three minutes.
There's no comparison.

Section VI

Six Critical Tips

A few weeks before I started law school, I had a fifteen-minute conversation with an old friend from college, Kevin Boon. At the time, he was a 2L at a prestigious law school in New York, and he frequently complained about his abusive professors and conniving peers. He sat me down on his couch and dropped a stack of books in my lap. He told me that they were called *supplements* and I needed to read them if I wanted to ace my exams.

"I don't care about this stuff," I said. "I'm just going to show up at law school and see what happens. I don't want to stress about anything now."

"Shut up," he said. "You're an idiot."

He then told me six things about law school, and his advice shaped my entire education. I've omitted the insults and swearing, but the advise is useful nonetheless.

Tip 1: Get Adjusted Quickly

Law School Is Unlike Anything You've Ever Done Before

Law professors teach and test with a very specific educational philosophy. Basically, they drop you in a 200-gallon shark tank, headfirst and blindfolded. If you swim to the surface, you get a gold medal. If you get chewed up, they will encourage the bits of you that remain to pull together and become accountants or English professors.[1]

Your professors aren't trying to torment you. They're actually trying to help you, even if some of their efforts are counterintuitive or downright misguided. The process is going to feel different from your other educational experiences, and you might not like it. Your early instinct will be to adapt your old skills as a student or a professional to this new environment. You should resist that feeling. For the first few months *don't fight the system, just go with it.* If your professor says to write a certain way, just do it. If she wants you to respond to questions in class in a particular strange manner, just play along. Everybody has to wear funny hats to class? No problem, point me to the hat store. Eventually you will learn how to bend the rules, but for the first few weeks of law school, just do what you are told. You need to learn the rules before you can bend them.

This Ain't Undergrad

The worst misjudgment you can make as a law student is treating law school like undergraduate college. The only 100% guarantee I can offer you is that your old study habits will not suffice. Cramming at the end of the semester is impossible, and you can't fake it on exam day. You are expected to understand the assigned material with much more precision and detail than you are accustomed to, and you need to keep a steady pace throughout the semester.

In Fact, Your Past Experience Can Hold You Back

Surprisingly, students with a background in writing or a law-related field (like real estate or criminal justice) tend to struggle more than most other students, and may underperform in their

---

1. Sound harsh? *See* Karl Llewellyn's famous book on the philosophy of legal education, *The Bramble Bush* for a brutal description of this philosophy.

first few exams. This is probably because those students *think* their prior experiences and skills give them an advantage in law school. As a result, they attempt to incorporate their old knowledge and habits into their new academic environment. By contrast, a high percentage of top students have no background in law or writing whatsoever.

Most likely, this is because students with no prior background in law approach the educational process as a blank slate. They just do whatever they are told. They don't resist, and they never think, "I know a better way to handle that issue in the real world."

If you've never gone to law school before, you don't know how to be a law student. You should embrace this ignorance. Be a blank slate. You came here to learn, and you will.

Tip 2: Prepare for Exams, Not for Class

One Big Test

In most classes, your entire grade will be based on a single exam at the end of the semester. You really only have one opportunity to earn your grade. As unpleasant as it may seem, get used to it. Think about what it means for your study routine.

"Don't Let Me Look Stupid!"

Since many professors aggressively ask questions in class, students tend to spend all of their daily study time on memorization. These students focus on the inane details of each case, out of fear that they will be called upon to recount the facts or holding in class. I call this the "please-don't-let-me-look-stupid-in-class" method.

If you're doing this, you should stop. In most courses, class participation accounts for about 5% of your final grade. On the other hand, your exam will account for the remaining 95%. No matter how badly you mess up when you are called on in class, it will have a miniscule effect on your grade.

Instead, you should be using your daily study time on preparing for the exam. Your notes from books and lectures should be aimed at producing a useful and personalized study-aid, which will help you prepare at the end of the semester. The cases should be understood in the perspective of your entire course. You need to see the rules as an intricate and interwoven mesh of concepts, not discrete bullet points to recite when called upon.

It really doesn't matter if you are prepared for next Tuesday's Torts class. The only thing that matters is your preparedness for the exam. That is your real opportunity to show the professor that you are not stupid. Cramming for class is a waste of time, especially if you won't even retain the information when it comes time for the exam.

Tip 3: You Will Frequently Feel Insecure

"I Am Completely Lost. Law School Was a Mistake"

If you are completely lost, you need to meet with the director of the law school's academic support program or someone at the Dean of Students' Office. Don't wait until you tank your first exam; talk to someone now. Reading this book might help, but hands-on support from a human being makes all the difference.

Lost *Is a Problem,* Confused *Is Normal*

Before you decide to drop out of law school, ask yourself if you are *totally lost* or just *really confused*. Take a look around at your classmates. Do the blank gazes, pallid complexions, and strings of drool look familiar? That's probably the same expression that greets you in the mirror each morning. *Nobody knows what's going on.* They all feel confused. Except for that annoying girl who raises her hand six times per hour. She's got it together, what's her deal?

Get used to a general feeling of confusion, anxiety, and discomfort because it will be with you for the next three years. If your head is spinning on a Tuesday afternoon in October, don't worry. Just keep working, and try to incorporate some of the advice from this book. If you stay on track, it will come together eventually.

You Can't Possibly Do Everything

Everybody's got two cents about law school. Friends, family, professors, and books like this—there's a lot of advice out there, and much of it is contradictory. One example is the undying debate among law school experts about whether briefing cases is important or pointless. There are successful students on both sides of the debate, so they can't all be right.

Trust yourself and use your own judgment. You can't possibly do everything that is suggested to you. If briefing cases helps you prepare for exams, you should do it. If it doesn't help, don't do it. Not sure yet? Try it for a while. The bottom line is, you have to use common sense when developing a strategy.

You may see one of your classmates memorizing a law dictionary and another with a ten-inch deck of flashcards. Don't worry; you don't have to do everything that your peers are doing. Make good decisions, incorporate good advice, and ignore distraction. You are learning something new, and it involves vulnerability and risk. Everyone's in the same boat and nobody really knows what to do. Sometimes, the best thing is to just trust your instincts.

Tip 4: Never Fall Behind in Your Assignments

Uh-oh, Time to Panic

If you are behind in any of your assigned readings, catching up should be your top priority. If a reading passage or case was assigned, it is fair game on the exam. You need to know all of it; every case, every concept. You won't have time to learn it all during a school recess, or reading period before the exam. Put down this book, cancel your weekend plans, and complete your missed reading assignments now. If you are very far behind, you should make a schedule of double or triple reading time for the next few weeks. It's going to be painful, but it is necessary.

Read Every "Topic" Not Every "Page"

You don't need to read every word on every page. That would be a waste of time, and very few successful law students even attempt it. Instead, you should think of your syllabus as a list of "topics" that you will be expected to know for the exam. You can learn these topics in a variety of ways (reading the casebook, using supplements, listening to class lectures, drilling with a study group, etc.). Most likely it will take some combination of resources to adequately prepare for your exam.

Your reading time should be spent with books that help you learn the material quickly, clearly, and without unnecessary effort. If your casebook isn't doing the job, find something else to read. Just make sure you don't miss any of the assigned topics as you go.

Tip 5: Learn How to Write Exam Answers

All of Your Effort Is Wasted If You Can't Write Solid Exam Answers

Most students who perform poorly on exams actually knew the substantive material, but failed to adequately demonstrate their knowledge in writing. Professors expect to see a specific and organized format, which lays out the arguments and counter arguments in a methodical manner. Unfortunately, they expect you to miraculously figure out this format on your own. Nobody at school is going to teach you how to do it (except perhaps an academic support program at your law school).

Writing exam answers is like playing a musical instrument—if you don't have natural-born talent you need a teacher and tons of practice. This book can be your teacher, but the practice has to come from you.

Tip 6: You Will Work 40% Harder Than You Expected

Relax, It's Not as Bad as It Sounds

During one of my seminars, I told a group of two hundred first-semester 1Ls that they should be working 40% harder. These jittery, caffeine-soaked, overachievers were terrified by my proclamation. Convinced that they were already working at their maximum capacity, many of them announced their intention to drop out of law school. It took the kind counseling of the director of academic support to calm them down, and thankfully nobody ended their legal career because of me.

Don't misunderstand. I'm not telling you to fill every moment of your day with law study. Don't start sleeping in shifts or develop an energy-drink addiction. Just mentally prepare yourself for what lies ahead. You think you're already pushed to the max, but you're not. You have a much higher capacity to work and learn than you realize.

Law school is hard, but thankfully, it is also short. If you want to perform at a very high level, it's going to get intense. You will feel like quitting. You need to anticipate that these feelings of defeat may come, but you can't give up. You knew it was going to be hard when you decided to come, but the reality is probably harder than you anticipated. It will be over before you know it and you will be glad that you put in the effort.

If you are starting to feel short of breath after reading this section, just take a deep breath. In fact, just forget that I said anything about working 40% harder. It's going to be fine. Don't worry. Just ... don't drop out. Ok? Hello? You still there?

Not Everyone Needs to Work Harder

If you are already down to four hours of sleep because you're up all night listening to bootlegged recordings of old Torts lectures, you do not need to work 40% harder. You are working too hard, and you need a better work strategy. You need 40% more sleep. This book will help you improve your study habits in order to free up some relaxation time.

Section VII

The Big Mistakes

There are a handful of common pitfalls that will sabotage your success on a final exam. Most underperforming students landed in one or more of these traps.

Mistake 1: Falling Behind in Your Reading

Excuse Me While I Beat This Dead Horse

I want to make this absolutely clear, so I will repeat myself. You need to get on schedule with your reading assignments. I know the reading assignments in law school are unreasonable sometimes. They feel impossible, but they are not. How are you supposed to find the time? Start by addressing mistake number 2.

Mistake 2: Partying Too Much

At Least Bring Your Books to the Bar

If you are a 1L you should not be out on Thursday night. In fact, you should not be out on Friday or Saturday night either. 1L year is the most important year of your legal education, and you can't afford to ruin it because of a great happy-hour at the local pub. Studying on the weekends is critical to your success. You need that time to stay on pace for the exam.

This advice sounds harsh because you are in a new place and making new friends. Don't you deserve an occasional break to unwind? But before going out, ask yourself, "How many breaks have I already taken this week? This month?"

That syllabus is twenty pages long for a reason: It's going to take all semester to complete the readings. A six-hour break that leaves you hung-over or exhausted the next day is really counter-productive. Have friends, have fun, but stay focused and don't sacrifice your studying for partying. That includes 2Ls and 3Ls too, especially if your grades are below expectation. You have to drop some of your old habits, at least temporarily.

Mistake 3: Trying to Learn "The Law"

Learning Is Bad! (Sort of)

You are going to learn about the law as you progress through law school. You might even remember a thing or two when you get out into the real world. But don't carry the naïve belief that law school is about learning the law.

There's No Such Thing as the Law

The abstract concept that people refer to as "the law" is actually a loose patchwork of constantly evolving cases and statutes. Everything you learn in law school will become obsolete, and much of it is inaccurate to begin with. You're not learning rules. You are developing a set of skills that will benefit you in future professional endeavors, like analytical insight, organized thinking, the ability to explain complex situations, and the ability to persuade others. You will develop these skills by learning how to write exams, not by memorizing cases.

"So, I Don't Need to Learn Anything?"

Don't misunderstand—it is essential to study all of the cases and rules that your teacher assigns. In fact, your professors expect that you will have total mastery of those things by the end of the semester. But never forget that you're going to be tested in essay format, based on a factual scenario. The rules standing alone are useless if you can't bring them to life and apply them in real-world situations.

Don't worry about answering questions in class, don't worry if some topics don't make sense yet—focus all your energy on exam preparation and everything will fall into place.

Mistake 4: Relying on Professors to Teach You

Not All Professors Are Created Equal

Some professors will guide you through the course and help you focus on the important material. Others will stimulate great class discussions but leave you confused about the fundamentals of the course. Unfortunately, there are also many professors who will abuse, confuse, and mislead you as they drag you unwillingly through the semester.

You Need to Take Control

When I was a law student, I didn't care which type of professor I had—their lesson plans and teaching style had no impact on my ability to get a top grade. Why? Like all good law students *I took personal responsibility for learning the material. I never relied on my professors to teach me <u>anything</u>.* If I had a great professor who selected a great casebook, that certainly made my life a lot easier. But if I had a horrible professor who made a seemingly simple course into a murky and confusing mess, I just tuned him out, and found another way to learn.

At the end of the day, you've got to know the assigned material inside-and-out. Your professor is not going to make the test easier to compensate for his lousy teaching. You have to take responsibility for your own exam performance by finding a better source. Often, a good commercial outline will untangle a difficult class and set you back on track.

The Blame Game

After grades come out, you'll hear lots of students saying, "I got a *C* because my professor was horrible. She didn't teach us anything." Well think about it: Somebody got an *A* in that class, right? That *A* student probably agrees with you—the professor didn't teach her anything. The difference is she didn't just sit around and wait for the professor to improve; she took her success into her own hands.

"But Didn't You Say Earlier That I Should Just Do Whatever My Professor Says?"

Yes, but that section was for brand new students at the start of their law school education. If you don't know the terrain, you can't just head off in your own direction. Initially, go with the flow. How can you judge the quality of a professor when you've never taken a law class before?

However, at a certain point in the semester a little voice will start whispering in the back of your mind: "You're not ready for your exam. This professor isn't helping, and this book makes no sense." When you hear that voice, it's time to start heading in a different direction.

Mistake 5: Not Taking Practice Exams

Taking Practice Exams Is by Far the Most Important Thing You Can Do with Your Time

Most students take a preparation course before taking the LSAT. They pay thousands of dollars and study for weeks, with the hopes that it will yield three extra points on that horrible exam. But the biggest benefit of an LSAT course is the opportunity to take practice tests. The tricks that those courses teach may or may not help, but practice will definitely improve your score.

Practice Makes Perfect (or at Least, Better)

Writing a law school exam essay is a unique skill, that requires a balance of reading comprehension, memory recall, factual analysis, argumentative writing, explanatory writing, and speed. The only way to master it is by taking dozens of practice tests throughout the semester. There is just no way around it.

Can't Write about It? Then You Don't Know It

If you can't write about a particular topic, that means *you don't understand it yet.* The best way to discover the gaps in your knowledge is by writing a practice exam answer. It doesn't take away from your substantive study time — it is substantive studying.

Now Comes the Moment of Judgment

Despite my strong encouragement and the obvious benefits of practicing, students always resist me on this particular point. No matter how much I expound the benefits of writing practice exams, many students just don't do it. My only guess is that a combination of fear and laziness is to blame. But I promise you will overcome both of these faults if you just *do practice exams.*

You're already thinking of excuses. You've probably come up with at least five since you started reading this page. Well I'm ready for them all. You have no excuse.

FAQ on Practice Exams (and the Most Common Lame Excuses for Avoiding Them)

- **"When should I start doing practice exams?"** If you are a first semester 1L, you should start doing practice exams about five or six weeks before the actual test. If you are a higher level student, you should begin doing practice exams immediately.

- **"I can't start doing practice exams yet, because we haven't covered enough material in class."** Yes you can. The main purpose of doing practice exams is to develop your writing and organizational skills. When you start practicing, your analysis can be partial, or even incorrect. That's ok. As you work, you will develop strategies and time management skills that are crucial to your ultimate success. Find practice essay questions that cover material that you've already learned, or just skip the parts that are unfamiliar.

- **"I can't start doing practice exams because I haven't memorized anything yet."** Yes you can. Even if your actual exam will be closed book, I always suggest that students take their first five practice exams open-book, with all their notes and supplements available. After writing several essays, you will find that certain concepts are frequently tested. Repeating the same analysis multiple times will help you memorize. Doing many practice exams will also help you identify the most "testable" topics in the course, which will significantly increase your focus when you study later on.

- **"This question says it was supposed to be completed in 30 minutes, but it took me almost two hours."** That's not a problem at all. You should begin by taking all of your practice exams untimed. Instead of worrying about the time limit, try to write your best possible answer. By writing carefully and taking the time to revise, you will figure out ways to explain the most frequently tested concepts in a concise and clear way. For example, you will see that almost every Torts exam requires you to explain negligence in an identical manner. After tackling a dozen negligence questions, the analysis will become routine, and you will write surprisingly fast.

- **"How many practice exams should I do?"** I suggest doing about one or two practice exams per week during the early period of preparation, and maybe three or four as the actual exam approaches. You can practice different subjects each week, or start by focusing on a course that feels a little easier. On the day before each exam, I suggest doing at least four or five practice essays.

- **"I can't do practice exams because my teacher hasn't given us any."** This is the most common and most lame excuse that I hear. First, check the circulation desk at the law library. Professors frequently provide a stash of old exams for students to photocopy. If your professor has not put any tests on reserve, you should ask her to do so.

  If you can't get any old exams from your professor, you're still not off the hook. Although actual past exams are best, almost any generic hypothetical will suffice for practice purposes. In the back of most commercial supplements, you will find several excellent practice essay exams with model answers. Additionally, you can use other exams from the library's reserve bank, even if they are from different professors.

  Right now, you are focused on developing your ability to answer a hypothetical, and it doesn't matter who wrote the question. The skills that you develop by practicing on generic exams will translate to the real exam, I promise.

- **"I don't have time to do practice exams. I'm too busy."** Writing practice essays is too important to ignore, so you need to find the time. You may have to reduce your reading time by using supplements, or cut out some leisure activities as final exams draw closer. You might even have to take a few "sick days" from school to grab some extra study-hours (just don't tell anyone I suggested it). Prioritize the activities that will maximize your exam performance.

- **"I'm a 2L reading this over summer break. Can I do practice exams now?"** Yes, do Torts exams. During my live seminars I make all the students practice with Torts exams, even 2Ls and 3Ls who have already taken that class. Why Torts? First, you probably had a pretty good grasp on the material in Torts and have managed to remember some of the basics. Second, the multi-issue fact patterns on the average Torts question are particularly good for practicing. Third, the skills you develop by practicing with *any* exam will translate to your current classes. If Torts wasn't your strongest course, pick another class that you felt more comfortable with.

Section VIII

Final Thoughts

I don't want to take up too much more of your time. You're much better off doing a practice exam than reading another one of my anecdotes. I just want to give you some parting words of advice — the most essential points to remember from this book.

Stay Caught Up

Keep up a good pace throughout the semester so you'll have room to breathe when it really counts later on. Remember, exam preparation takes all semester. My grandfather used to say "Pay now, or pay later." You can't escape from hard work, eventually it will catch up with you.

Don't Give Up

Law school is difficult. You're not the only one that's struggling. Keep working.

Don't Be Afraid to Take Risks

Let's say you are eight weeks into the semester and you realize that all of your Civil Procedure notes are completely useless. When you began the semester they seemed good enough, but now you can see that they are wholly inadequate for exam preparation. You are faced with a difficult decision: Continue with what you've already started, or throw it all away and start over.

There's no clear answer, and it might work out well either way. But don't let laziness or fear guide your decision. Sometimes the right choice will be to abandon your work and try something totally new. Don't be afraid of this option. It may feel like you've wasted half the semester, but you haven't. You should be thankful that the inadequate technique led you to something more efficient. You won't make the same mistake again, and that knowledge will benefit you on all future exams.

Take Personal Responsibility for Learning

I have great respect and affection for all of my law school professors. Don't get the wrong impression from my occasional jokes on their behalf. But liking or disliking a professor has very little to do with learning. You have to take 100%, unconditional, personal responsibility for learning everything in law school. That includes learning how to please your professors and their individual idiosyncrasies. You can't just sit back and be a passenger in law school. You must take control of the educational process.

Do Practice Exams

If you really want to succeed, all it takes is practice. After about ten practice exams, you will have a whole new perspective on law school. You can ignore every tip, trick, and tactic in this book— just do as many practice exams as you can.

Be More than a GPA

I know you don't want to hear philosophical life lessons right now. You bought this book to boost your GPA, and there's nothing wrong with that. I just want to remind you that there's more to life than grades. You've got a long career ahead of you, and it's going to twist and turn in unexpected ways. The most important personal and professional events in your life will probably be unplanned. They have been in mine.

Law school was a time of great fraternity and intellectual engagement for me. It was also extremely difficult and showed me a lot about myself as a person. Try to appreciate the experience, because it is really something special.

I hope that you enjoyed this book. Good luck.